NEW
MANAGERS

HarperCollins
LEADERSHIP
AN IMPRINT OF HarperCollins

NEW MANAGERS

MASTERING THE BIG THREE PRINCIPLES
OF EFFECTIVE MANAGEMENT—LEADERSHIP,
COMMUNICATION, AND TEAMBUILDING

PAUL FALCONE

Published by HarperCollins Leadership, an imprint of HarperCollins Focus LLC.

Published in association with Kevin Anderson & Associates: https://www.ka-writing.com/.

Topic 11: From "Why Senior Managers Should Hold Skip-Level Meetings." *SHRM HR Daily Newsletter*, May 31, 2018. Copyright 2018 by the Society for Human Resource Management. **Topic 19:** From "How to Bridge Cultural Divides." *SHRM HR Daily Newsletter*, August 27, 2020. Copyright 2020 by the Society for Human Resource Management. **Topic 23:** From "Dealing with Employees in Crisis: Options and Resources for Today's Turbulent Times." *SHRM HR Daily Newsletter*, November 23, 2020. Copyright 2020 by the Society for Human Resource Management. **Topic 24:** From "What All Senior Executives Wish Their Front-Line Managers Knew About Effective Leadership." *SHRM HR Daily Newsletter*, June 3, 2016. Copyright 2016 by the Society for Human Resource Management. **Topic 25:** From "Viewpoint: How to Practice Inspirational Leadership." *SHRM HR Daily Newsletter*, January 16, 2019. Copyright 2019 by the Society for Human Resource Management. All of the above used by permission of the publisher. All rights reserved.

Any internet addresses, phone numbers, or company or product information printed in this book are offered as a resource and are not intended in any way to be or to imply an endorsement by HarperCollins Leadership, nor does HarperCollins Leadership vouch for the existence, content, or services of these sites, phone numbers, companies, or products beyond the life of this book.

This book is written as a source of information only. The information contained in this book should by no means be considered a substitute for the advice, decisions, or judgment of the reader's professional advisors.

All efforts have been made to ensure the accuracy of the information contained in this book as of the date published. The author and the publisher expressly disclaim responsibility for any adverse effects arising from the use or application of the information contained herein.

ISBN 978-1-4002-3015-0 (eBook)
ISBN 978-1-4002-3006-8 (TP)

Library of Congress Control Number: 2021951254

Printed in the United States of America
22 23 24 25 26 LSC 10 9 8 7 6 5 4 3 2 1

CONTENTS

Introduction: For First-Time Managers........................ ix

PART 1

▪ Leadership and Becoming a "Favorite Boss":
The Ultimate in Job Satisfaction 1

1. How to Become a Favorite Boss............................3
2. Leading Through Coaching................................8
3. Coaching and Mentoring Rests on the Questions You Ask 12
4. Inspiring Employee Engagement 17
5. The Coin of the Realm: Trust............................ 20
6. The Big Benefits of Laughter in the Workplace.............. 25

PART 2

▪ Better Communication Leads to Better Management............ 29

7. Master the Art of Engaged Listening...................... 31
8. The Art of Successful Communication:
Simple Guidelines to Help Your Messages Soar 35
9. Three Steps to Great Staff Meetings...................... 44
10. Facilitating Information Sharing:
Quarterly Achievement Calendars 49
11. Skip-Level Meetings Help Managers Communicate
with Employees Who Aren't Direct Reports................. 52

12. Confrontation Is a Necessary Part of Communication 57
13. Tough Conversations:
Your Moral Obligation to Confront Constructively 64
14. Encouraging Someone to Leave Your Company by Resigning:
When It's Right for You and Right for Them 70

PART 3
■ Teambuilding 79

15. The Importance of Teamwork,
Camaraderie, and Cooperation 81
16. Helping Your Team Learn, Grow,
and Develop Professionally 86
17. Delegation as a Means of Team Development:
Good for You, Good for Your Team 90
18. Remote Leadership: Managing the Unseen 94
19. Managing Multiple Generations of Employees:
Raising Awareness of Others' Perspectives
and Points of View 100
20. The Importance of Fostering
a Diverse and Inclusive Workforce 107

PART 4
■ Putting It All Together 111

21. Establishing Key Metrics to Drive Your Business 113
22. How HR and Frontline Managers Can Work
Together to Reduce Employee Turnover 119
23. Dealing with Employees in Crisis:
A Blueprint for Positive Management Intervention 124

24. What Got You Here Won't Get You There:
Assess Yourself to Become a Better Manager 132
25. Inspirational Leadership: Some Final Thoughts 135

Index. 139
About the Author. 147

INTRODUCTION
FOR FIRST-TIME MANAGERS . . .

Welcome to book 5 of the *Paul Falcone Workplace Leadership Series*. This is the fifth and final book in the series and is special because it's uniquely tailored to the needs of new managers and frontline supervisors. Newly minted managers often experience a unique set of problems that, once mastered, won't likely challenge them again to the same degree. But that's because they'll garner the necessary experiences to master the supervision of others by then. Still, the first time can be tricky and somewhat uncomfortable as new managers get used to their new level of leadership and authority, especially if they naturally feel a bit overwhelmed by the thought of it all.

Why the Big Three? Ask most CEOs what they expect from their management teams, and you'll hear about effective leadership, excellent communication skills, talent development, ethical and moral behavior, adaptability to change, high accountability for self and others, and so much more. But if you take the full list of attributes and talents and boil them down to the top three competencies on CEOs' short lists, then leadership, communication, and teambuilding win every time.

Yes, quite a lot is asked of newly promoted managers, not the least of which is that often they must remain solid individual contributors, willing to roll up their sleeves and produce (and sometimes out-produce) their team members in terms of both volume and quality. It's rare to have a pure leadership position these days, even when you head your own department! But mastering leadership takes time and focus. Sure, there are "born leaders" out there, but even if you considered yourself a leader since your very first day in kindergarten, there are still so many rules, practices, and yes—land mines—that await the unsuspecting manager that you really need to hone your craft and choose your allies well.

Education is always your first go-to resource. This book, for example, touches on topics as varied as internal coaching and employee engagement to motivation and career development as well as diversity awareness and managing multiple generations at work. It also contains healthy doses of information on self-assessment, dealing with employees in crisis, and becoming an inspirational leader.

Of course, all five books in the series are dedicated to strengthening leadership muscle, whether in the form of ethical decision-making (book 1), effective interviewing and hiring (book 2), leadership offense (book 3), and leadership defense (book 4). But book 5, which you're holding in your hands right now, is meant to pull everything together in one place, inspiring you to become a trusted leader, a strategic thinker, and a deliverer of high impact results.

No book or book series can capture all the variances of effective leadership. But the content that follows will help you build confidence and trust in your abilities, master the art of the internal coach (rather than the unilateral disciplinarian), confront problematic issues head-on in a caring and constructive manner, and develop your own unique management and leadership style. More important, it will help you avoid some of the pitfalls and snares that can otherwise entangle a well-intentioned leader who "just didn't see something coming." Rest assured that this author has your back, understands the unique pressures and challenges you face, and has every confidence that your commitment to self-education and self-awareness will reward you with incredible dividends over time.

Leadership is the greatest gift that the workplace has to offer: nothing else gives you the opportunity to touch others' lives, to pay it forward, to become their favorite boss, and ultimately to be thanked years later for contributing to a team member's success. Enjoy your new role and the exciting opportunities it creates. Listen with your heart, laugh a lot, recognize and appreciate others, and always come from a spirit of thankfulness and gratitude. After all, appreciation of the many opportunities you have—and the people you serve as a leader—opens your whole world to greater and higher levels of success and self-fulfillment.

Congratulations for mastering the course to this point in your career: you've achieved your management stripes. As we'll soon see, however, management and leadership are two separate things, and leadership should always be what you strive for: the ability to positively influence others, to motivate and engage them, to bring out their best, and to help them grow and develop in their own careers. Once you get the groove of this, you'll see that it's easier to master than you might have originally thought. Choose your mentors well, partner closely with your boss at all times, keep HR in the loop as your loyal sidekick and internal guidance resource, and know with confidence that your organization and your team can benefit tremendously from your leadership contributions.

I'm so happy you chose me and this book to help get you there. Let's launch into your leadership and management career together. I'm so looking forward to joining you on this new journey and hopefully assisting you in becoming the greatest leader you can be, both for your own good as well as the good of all those you'll serve successfully in the future. Now let's get going—we've got a lot to cover!

DISCLAIMER

Note: Throughout this book, I interchange the use of *his* and *her,* and I provide examples of fictitious men and women. Obviously, all situations described in these pages can apply to anyone. Further, please bear in mind at all times that this book is not intended as a legal guide. Because the book does not purport to render legal advice, it should not be used in place of a licensed practicing attorney when proper legal counsel and guidance become necessary. You must rely on your attorney to render a legal opinion that is related to actual fact situations.

LEADERSHIP AND BECOMING A "FAVORITE BOSS"

THE ULTIMATE IN JOB SATISFACTION

HOW TO BECOME A FAVORITE BOSS

When you ask people about their favorite bosses, their eyes light up and they say things like:

She always made me feel like she had my back.

He challenged me to do things I didn't think I was capable of.

She made me feel included, she appreciated my input, and I felt like I could almost do no wrong when working with her. My confidence soared.

These descriptions focus on who that person *is*, not necessarily what that person *did*. It's leaders' *beingness*, no *doingness*, that makes them great. In other words, change your focus from "What I am doing?" to "Who am I being?" at any given time when it comes to effectively leading others. Respect, sincerity, and selflessness are all a function of your beingness; if you come from that healthy perspective, you'll naturally *do* all the things that make great leaders great. So, as a new manager, the first question to ask yourself should be, "Who am I, and who do I choose to be in light of this concept called *management* and *leadership*?" Likewise, remember that it is leadership *through,* not management *over,* that should be your goal. Your ability to expand your personal impact on your organization grows exponentially when given the honor to serve—and lead—others to success. From this point forward, your individual success is measured by the performance and productivity of your team. Now that's an exciting concept!

As we prepare to launch our journey into leadership and management, let's start with the end goal in mind. Look to American poet Maya Angelou's famous words as guideposts to your own leadership style: "People will forget what you said, people will forget what you did, but people will never forget how you made them feel." Think about it: Would you want to work for you? If the whole company followed your lead, would you be happy with where you took it? To quote spiritual author Neale Donald Walsch, what you want for yourself, give to another. Teach what you choose to learn. And when in doubt, err on the side of compassion. It's that simple. And leadership can be that much more meaningful and rewarding when you're both modeling leadership behaviors and conduct for others and paying it forward by growing future generations of leaders in their own right. This, then, is the essence of successful leadership, the mindset you need going forward to influence those you're privileged to serve. Selfless leadership is your goal, which we'll explore in its many facets throughout this book.

Especially in times of crisis—whether it's a financial crisis, a global pandemic, or something specific to your industry or business—new managers drive the way forward. You need to maintain open communication, build a stronger team (especially if you're working remotely), and produce and measure performance results. In times of crisis or change, you face additional challenges—for example:

■ loss of safety and security
■ loss of control due to unpredictable events
■ lack of emotional and social support (and feelings of loneliness and isolation)
■ loss of peers and friends due to unexpected turnover
■ overwork, exhaustion, or lack of self-care

You need to not only manage performance but also demonstrate the soft skills of listening, empathy, and genuine concern for your employees. Here's what your communication and leadership strategy might focus on during difficult times:

■ Communicate organizational resources, like your organization's employee assistance program (EAP), or local resources such as pastoral care and social services.
■ Be a calming influence for your team by introducing moments of pause or meditation.
■ Form "battle-buddy" relationships. Pair up remote team members and ensure that people have each other's backs at all times and feel connected to one another.
■ Help people change their perspective so they'll change their perception of current events. Talk about how this, too, shall pass. Take your people out of the weeds and up to the thirty-thousand-foot level so they can see and appreciate the broader changes at hand. Encourage people to think about where we will be one to five years from now when we look back on this time. How can your team use this period to develop their careers and skills? How can they turn lemons into lemonade?

It's also important to motivate employees so they can focus on the work itself because striving to meet goals—and achieving those goals—helps build confidence. Help your people become resume builders by codifying their accomplishments and developing an achievement mindset. To that end, follow some of these best practices when leading your team, either in person or remotely:

- Create a shared document where everyone on the team can document their weekly progress, roadblocks, and achievements. Use it for celebration and recognition.
- Assign different staff members to lead weekly staff meetings and make them responsible for the agenda and follow-up items.
- Catch people being good: recognition and appreciation for a job well done provide the "psychic income" that's so important for people to thrive in their roles.
- Schedule quarterly progress meetings on annual goals, roadblocks, and achievements as well as career and professional goals (using what are known as IDPs, or individual development plans).
- Seek to increase awareness of diversity and inclusion, multigenerational communication, and the importance of laughter and camaraderie in the workplace.
- Ensure that remote workers' work-life balance needs are being met (for example, by not working all hours of the night) and that nonexempt employees adhere strictly to wage and hour guidelines for meal and rest periods as well as overtime.

More than ever, people are looking to their leaders and managers in business to respond quickly and proactively. This is the time to lean in, lead through the changes coming your way, show compassion for others, exercise the selflessness necessary to coach and mentor, and ensure high levels of individual and team performance. Help your employees process their physical and mental reactions stemming from fear and uncertainty and focus on performance, productivity, and shared achievements. Redefine your leadership and communication style so that others look to you as that special boss; that individual who taught them how to lead, pivot, and bend through a crisis; and that leader who had their backs and encouraged them to discover their personal best through challenging times. Remember that the greatest leaders are not the ones with the most followers; they're the ones who create the most leaders in turn. You can be that inspirational leader, that transformative leader, that turnaround leader for others. And in doing so, you'll develop the greatest level of career satisfaction possible. The opportunity to lead and manage is an opportunity to touch others' lives and pay it forward like no other in the workplace. Mastering leadership begins and ends with becoming someone's favorite boss. With that concept in mind, let's figure out together how to get this done.

2

LEADING THROUGH COACHING

The strongest leaders are coaches, not disciplinarians. They are self-less teachers who take personal interest in their employees' professional growth and career development. They see leadership as a gift and as the greatest privilege the workplace has to offer. After all, what other endeavors in the business world, beyond compensation, are as significant as hearing that you're someone's favorite boss, the person who influenced and shaped them to become the best leaders they could become in their own right, and their role models and greatest influencers in their careers? Becoming a people developer may not be the first thing that comes to mind in your role as a leader, executive, manager, or supervisor. But it may be time to focus on building that particular leadership muscle because you want to, not because you have to. In fact, that's likely why you purchased this book or book series! Now let's take a quick look under the hood to see how it can be accomplished.

First, great leadership is about sincerity and selflessness. The old paradigm of the "boss" dictating what to do and how to get it done from the top down—that is, the traditional role of *management*—has been replaced by the *leadership* concept. Management is about oversight, control, and order, leaving little discretion to the individual laborer. Competence, compliance, and the appropriate balance of power are critical. Traditional managers embrace process and try to resolve problems quickly by making unilateral decisions and "giving orders" that achieve immediate results. And yes, there is still a need for the traditional management paradigm in the workplace, depending on the type of work to be done.

Leadership is different. It has a different focus and feel. And it tends to get much greater results over time because compliance will never get you more than 100 percent of employee effort (if that much)—people will do their jobs but only go so far in terms of the energy they expend.

Leadership, in comparison, favors consensus over individual decision-making. It looks for inspiration, imagination, creativity, and ethical behavior in piercing workers' hearts as well as their minds. It thrives on respect, inclusiveness, and a culture of otherness that permits and rewards selfless leadership and emotional intelligence. The optimal result is that selfless leaders gain additional effort from their team members—a willingness to go above and beyond 100 percent because of the love and trust they have in their leader. This is commonly referred to as *discretionary effort*.

For example, becoming a favorite boss was discussed in book 2 of this series on interviewing and hiring. It can start at the applicant interview stage, by simply amending your interview questioning style to include the following questions to open the door to a heightened sense of selfless leadership and career development:

What's important to you at this point in your career, and what two or three criteria are you using to select your next job opportunity or role?

If you were to accept this position with us, based on your current understanding of the role, how would this help you build your resume and LinkedIn profile in terms of your longer-term career goals?

Likewise, if you were to accept an offer to join our organization, how might you explain that to a prospective employer three to five years from now? In other words, how would this role serve as a link toward your career progression?

Next, understand that excellent leaders ask questions of their employees even when they already know the answers. The questioning process is used to teach. And yes—it may take longer than simply giving the right answer—but it's important for your team members' professional development. You've probably heard of managers who say:

Whenever you have a question or challenge, bring me two to three possible solutions that you've thought through so we can discuss them together.

The question I like to use is a bit more flippant and fun:

I know you don't know the answer, *but if you did know,* what would it be?

This forces employees to proffer a solution on the spot, and more often than not, you'll find that their answers and recommendations are fairly close to what you would have recommended in the first place. At that point, you can ask a few follow-up questions to tease the correct answer out of them or help them course correct to reach the answer on their own with your guided help.

Finally, strong "coaching leaders" meet with their employees at least quarterly to spend one-on-one time reviewing performance goals, removing roadblocks, pivoting in light of unforeseen challenges, and asking questions about professional growth and development.

What can I do to provide you with more structure, direction, and feedback to help you meet your personal and professional goals?

How can I support you in terms of furthering your education, certification, licensure, or professional development?

How can I help you expand your professional network, build stronger technical muscle, or help you gain more organizational exposure?

What are you focusing on now to build your resume and LinkedIn profile?

How are you measuring your achievements and accomplishments and turning them into bullets for your quarterly and annual reviews?

Such are the questions and interests of great leaders. And you'll likely find that there will be little turnover on your team when your interests focus so strongly on theirs.

The leader-as-coach model looks to draw wisdom, insight, and creativity from the people being coached. It focuses on teaching people to fish rather than simply giving them a fish. It encourages them to resolve problems they have thought through with the underlying assumption that the answer is in them already and simply needs to be guided out. Coaching others to high performance is a noble goal and will likely catapult your own reputation as a people leader and talent developer. Never underestimate the power of being a strong team builder: it could open more opportunities for you career-wise than you might otherwise imagine.

3

COACHING AND MENTORING
RESTS ON THE QUESTIONS YOU ASK

C oaching and mentoring employees is a critical aspect of effective leadership, and it all hinges on appropriate communication. Let's look at coaching and mentoring—your opportunity to train and develop those employees who are following in your footsteps or otherwise growing and developing in their own respective careers—and the questions that help people thrive.

When people feel valued, acknowledged, and appreciated, they will typically respond with increased commitment and enthusiasm, which naturally translates into higher productivity. Even though performance reviews typically occur only once a year, most experts in the field of leadership and management (including me) will argue that the optimal amount of time devoted to formal performance feedback is four hours per year or one hour per quarter. This is a fourfold increase over what most companies do and what most workers experience, but the strongest leaders provide formal feedback four times per year to catch up on progress, redefine goals in light of new information, and provide timely updates and guidance to their team members.

So how do you coach and develop your employees throughout the year in ways that will lead to a highly fueled, self-aware, and engaged team? To structure your conversations, make sure they are:

1. *Specific:* Use real examples. Detailed feedback that is recent and "real" becomes actionable and much more meaningful to the recipient.

2. *Balanced:* People need to hear both what they are doing well and where they need to improve. The age-old advice still holds: you will garner much greater results as a leader if you spend your time and energy building people's strengths rather than managing their weaknesses. It's likewise true that, as a leader, you will be better off focusing on people's natural talents and encouraging them to become more of who they already are rather than on trying to fix their weaknesses or making them perfect. That's what teams are all about—diverse groups of individuals with varying strengths and talents who complement one another so that the whole is greater than the sum of its parts. Still, hearing both positive and encouraging information in addition to areas of development and opportunity provides a balanced approach to coaching and mentoring, because employees generally want more input to focus on their self-development and heighten their self-awareness.

3. *Timely:* Waiting months to deliver feedback dilutes its impact and sends the message that the matter wasn't especially important. Providing actual, real-time feedback between formal performance intervals should become a matter of practice and expectation. The ongoing feedback loop will garner you high points as a caring leader who's focused on

employee development. Also, don't be afraid to shift the responsibility for timely feedback back to your employees: simply instruct them to call intermittent update meetings to discuss their progress and keep you informed of any surprises along the way—pleasant or otherwise.

4. *Continual:* In the same way we need to keep our cars fueled with gas, we need to keep our people fueled with feedback. That's the psychological oxygen that keeps them engaged and refreshed, and it removes any awkwardness when it comes to addressing minor issues before they escalate. After all, if feedback is ongoing and continual, then it simply becomes an expectation and a given under your leadership.

Likewise, when meeting with an employee whom you're mentoring or coaching, ask questions such as the following:

Do you have a clear understanding of what's expected of you at work?

Could you articulate what would garner a "meets expectations" score on your annual review versus an "exceeds expectations" or "superior" rating for your particular role?

Do you have the materials, equipment, and training that you need to be successful?

What's your biggest concern currently?

Do you feel that your opinion counts and that you have a voice on our team?

If you could change one thing right now that would make things better for us as a team or how we get our work done, what would it be?

Do you feel you have adequate opportunities to learn and grow in your role? Are there any types of rotational or stretch assignments that you feel could help you progress in your career more effectively?

These questions are easily customized, of course, but the examples above should help you launch into a conversation fairly seamlessly. More important than the particular questions you ask is your sincere interest in the individual's growth and development.

Whether you're delivering coaching and recognition for a job well done or directly addressing problematic performance or conduct issues that may arise from time to time, remember that being a great communicator doesn't mean only delivering good news. It also means delivering challenging news in a positive and constructive manner. Great leaders are great communicators, and there are few areas that you could invest in that will yield greater results than becoming a stellar and transparent communicator and coach.

ABOLISH ANNUAL PERFORMANCE REVIEWS? I THINK NOT!

Don't get lost in the hype about annual performance appraisals being a waste of time, a net demotivator, or a paperchase with no meaningful purpose. As we discuss in book 3, *Leadership Offense,* annual reviews make total sense unless they're issued in a vacuum and then tucked away in a filing cabinet till the following year. Annual reviews are the natural result of quarterly IDP (individual development plan) meetings where company, department, and individual goals are set. Those goals may be adjusted quarterly during your one-on-one IDP meetings with your team members where you discuss goal status and career progression. Just as publicly traded companies issue quarterly (10Q) reports that feed the annual (10K) report, individual performance and career discussion junctures should happen regularly (and ideally at quarterly intervals) throughout the year.

And no, there's not an app for that. While apps may help provide real-time feedback and on-the-spot peer recognition and appreciation, apps were never designed to deliver negative news. That can only be done with a human touch.

INSPIRING EMPLOYEE ENGAGEMENT

Another challenge often facing new managers is how to motivate employees when your organization may have a limited amount of dollars for salary increases, few promotional opportunities, and daunting workloads that demand high levels of discretionary effort. What about when layoffs loom: How can new managers keep staffers engaged when a sense of gloom pervades the workplace? More broadly, how do you foster respect and loyalty and exhibit role-model behavior in light of the challenges facing your company from time to time?

Becoming a leader who inspires team members by example and who creates an environment in which people can motivate themselves stems from building trust, respect, and camaraderie in the workplace. The keys to motivating and engaging those who report to you lies first in assessing your relationship with your employees, engaging in "stay interviews" with your top performers to ensure that they're energized and in tune with your department's and company's overall goals, and helping your team members build their skills and success profiles to prepare for their next move in career progression—whether at your organization or elsewhere.

Yes, you read that right: whether at your organization *or elsewhere*.

Selfless leadership (also known as servant leadership) requires putting your team members' needs above your own and expecting them to respond in kind. There's no doubt, however, that garnering loyalty and getting people to fall in love with your company stems not only from engaging their heads but from piercing their hearts. True motivation is inspirational and emotional—not necessarily logical or cognitive. Knowing that there are ways to win people's hearts as well as their minds will provide you with a special formula to foster respect and loyalty throughout your career.

Whether you're an introvert or extrovert, a driver, an analyst, or a people pleaser, the following steps foster greater employee commitment and dedication:

- Get to know your team members individually and personally.
- Give meaning to their work.
- Demonstrate respect and trust in all you do.

The key question, of course, is how do you accomplish this with the members of your team at any given time? How can you reach a level of engagement at which people feel valued, garner the appropriate amount of psychic income that comes from the workplace experience, and feel they're making a positive difference and that their opinion matters? On the one hand, this isn't as hard as you think if you apply certain principles and guidelines to engage and motivate winning teams. On the other hand, it can appear to be a most daunting task if leadership is new to you and you feel like you're trying to establish and balance yourself within this new discipline.

As a leader in corporate America, you're not (technically) responsible for motivating others. Motivation is internal, and employees must motivate themselves. But as a new manager and leader in your organization, you *are* responsible for creating a work environment where people can motivate themselves. There's a tremendous difference between creating the right working conditions versus crawling inside your team members' hearts and hoping to make them feel a certain way.

Now here's the good part: all you have to do is ask. Much of this book focuses on specific questions to ask in particular circumstances. But don't forget the importance of open-ended questions that simply ask, "What works best for you? How can I create the optimal work environment for you to not only succeed but to thrive?" Simply asking is enough. It creates transparency and trust, and those are critical elements in any new or existing relationship.

Further, what engages one employee won't mean much to another. So, common human interest will drive you to get to know each of your direct reports more personally. Not "personally" in the sense of being a friend or a peer: there should always be some level of tangible distance between you and those you manage. But "personally" in terms of your sincere interest in what's important to them at this point in their career and how you can help them help themselves in getting there. Natural curiosity will help you find the right questions under particular circumstances where your team members need your help: you simply need to make yourself available to them and to maintain an "open door" policy, so they feel welcome seeking your guidance and advice. Great leaders are flexible; leadership itself is fluid. Simply listen. You'll find that you'll gain confidence and trust the more you're there to mentor and coach them or point them to the appropriate resources and training when they need support.

5

THE COIN OF THE REALM
TRUST

The first rule for creating a motivated and engaged workforce is to practice open communication and transparency. The second rule is to provide recognition and appreciation to your staff as an integral part of your organizational strategy. While this may sound like common sense, common sense isn't often common practice.

What stops leaders from creating an environment where workers can feel fully engaged, self-motivated, and comfortable? Here are some excuses that managers typically use for not recognizing and rewarding their employees consistently:

I don't have the time.

I don't know what to do or what to say.

It's not an important part of my job—they can figure it out for themselves.

I don't want it to go to people's heads—they may want a promotion or a raise.

The company doesn't support or care about this—my boss rarely acknowledges me.

While these excuses may seem valid under certain circumstances, they provide a smoke screen or an easy out that ignores the needs of the team members. Everyone wants to know when they're doing a good job. A pat on the back by the boss—especially if called out in front of the rest of them—goes a long way in keeping employees engaged and invested. It's not that hard. And it's no excuse to say that no one does that for you. This is your shop now! You create the reality that you want to experience, regardless of what's happening above or around you.

Following is a simple short list of activities that tend to build and strengthen trust:

- Get to know your team members more personally, particularly via their goal-setting exercises, and maintain a proverbial open door to encourage them to seek your guidance.
- Emphasize a continual focus on career growth and development.
- Practice MBWA (management by walking around).
- Provide new recognition opportunities and celebrate successes grandly.
- Make others feel welcome, included, and heard.
- Praise in public by instituting "applause" bulletin boards or "wall of fame" photos for special achievers.
- Invest in experimental incentives, such as going-green initiatives, finding new ways of giving back to the community, and instituting health and wellness programs.
- Know members of your company by name (to the extent possible).
- Model the behaviors that you expect others to follow.

Successful leaders also practice open-book management (OBM), which entails sharing specifics about the company's financials in an attempt to get everyone on board with practical solutions to help the business. The basic tenet of OBM is that employees empowered with information and intelligence about the company not only perform their roles better but also gain a stronger understanding of how the company operates as a whole. The goal is to make employees partners in the business, offering solutions to challenges that may not be in their immediate purview. Yet who better than those in the trenches to recognize and flag potential problems in product manufacturing, service delivery, or the customer experience?

Further, when employees are given access to information and are involved in finding solutions to problems, they experience a greater sense of trust in the company and confidence in their managers. What better way to build and develop staffers than by educating them about your organization's challenges? What better way to keep people engaged and focused than by encouraging them to solve problems and suggest alternatives? Furthermore, learning about the financial drivers of organizational success helps build awareness of financial statements and ties team members' roles to the organization's bottom line.

To do this, you must first create an environment built on trust where it's safe to volunteer new ideas. Second, there must be a respectful and inclusive work environment where all workers are valued regardless of pay grade or title. Third, there must be some kind of critical measurement that is fairly easy to explain and that all employees can work toward. Whether you're sharing financial statements, feedback from an employee opinion survey, C-SAT (customer satisfaction survey) results, KPIs (key performance indicators), or scorecards, the more you inform, the more you educate. And the more you educate, the more people feel inspired to participate in finding solutions.

Start by picking a small task and introducing it as a new challenge. Discuss opportunities for influencing the critical measurement that's identified up front and encourage the sharing of ideas publicly. There are no right or wrong answers in this type of work environment—only suggestions for improvement. It may take the form of recruiters seeking to lower their hiring costs, insurance adjusters seeking to shorten the time it takes to close a claim, or organizations seeking to minimize their unemployment or disability expenses. But it's not just about efficiency and lowering costs. It's also about finding opportunities to increase revenue and introduce new marketing ideas. Are the employees the first users of new company products? Do all team members subscribe to your company's social media pages? Can your team members become due diligence experts and learn what competitor organizations are doing differently that may be worth considering? Are there opportunities to reinvent the way your organization does business, from the smallest detail to the largest initiative?

You'll only know if you ask. You can only ask if people feel truly safe to speak their minds and volunteer new ideas. But the art of employee retention is no longer strictly about job satisfaction: it's about true employee engagement. Involving employees in problem-solving, trusting workers to participate in activities or decisions that are beyond their immediate pay grade, and creating a learning environment where those in the trenches who are closest to the customer experience have a voice and can express their ideas will garner the highest results. That's the margin of difference that helps individual teams and entire companies stand out from their competition.

Foster a healthy sense of curiosity. Recognize that intrinsic motivation means that the interest comes naturally from within and that your job as an effective leader is to encourage that sense of inquisitiveness and help others tease out answers to challenges that require collaborative thought. As with many things in life, what matters is how you set things up and how you establish and communicate expectations. It's okay to start small and measure progress incrementally. Now the only questions are when do you start and what do you choose to share?

THE BIG BENEFITS OF
LAUGHTER IN THE WORKPLACE

The topic of fun and laughter in the workplace can make some readers cringe. After all, who hasn't experienced a jokester who just wasn't funny or, worse, someone who made others uncomfortable with their potentially offensive one-off comments? So, let's get that eight-hundred-pound gorilla out of the way as we open this subject: obviously, not *every* kind of humor is appropriate. When representing your company, locker room banter and bathroom humor, political, sexist, malicious, religious, homophobic, and xenophobic humor are big no-no's. (I'm a human resources practitioner, after all!)

Okay, fair enough. But don't discount the value and potential of healthy humor in the workplace. They say "laughter is the best medicine" for a reason. A healthy culture known for humor and lightheartedness produces incredible benefits, including:

- Creating an atmosphere of levity and a sense of perspective that can dissolve tension and, in turn, protect us from stress at work and improve our physical and mental health

- Keeping your team connected and bonded, especially when you're facing challenging times, so that people are more inclined to have others' backs
- Making team members more open to change, as the very act of laughing releases feel-good hormones that enhance concentration and creativity
- Driving greater innovation because employees who relax around one another and benefit from a playful culture are less concerned about making mistakes and open to taking risks—a foundation for finding more creative and innovative solutions at work
- Strengthening trust in management and fostering a greater sense of belonging and contentedness at work

A hint of self-deprecating humor can also be a useful tool for leaders and other employees to make themselves more approachable. In fact, when leaders and employees share a certain level of self-effacing banter, employees tend to gain even more professional respect for them—a counterintuitive finding for leaders who are afraid to show weakness. (Read that: it's okay to be human; everything doesn't always have to be perfect.)

Moreover, research suggests that people who engage in more conversational humor with colleagues feel happier and experience higher job satisfaction. For some reason, however, some managers see productivity and performance as the antithesis of fun. Along with it, laughter has become synonymous with wasting time. What's clear, though, is that corporate America suffers from an epidemic of being overly serious. That makes people miserable, and so it ends up taking a toll on productivity, creativity, and relationships in the workplace. Companies spend gobs of money on annual meetings, corporate retreats, and teambuilding activities in the hopes of spiking productivity and driving results that ultimately improve the bottom line. Laughter is a simpler (and cheaper) way to get there.

With all of the benefits to having humor in the workplace, every office could stand to have a little more fun if it wants to improve workplace productivity and happiness at work overall. But how do you incorporate humor into the corporate world? If we accept the premise that colleagues who laugh more together tend to enjoy a safer or more comfortable environment and a greater sense of cohesion, then it's best to determine how this might show itself in your workplace. Many of the ideas below will depend on your own personality and willingness to adopt a broader spirit of fun, but here are some places to start:

1. *Smile:* That's it, and it's that simple. Ask your team to just smile more. That's an order.

2. *Set Up Eat-and-Greets:* Start a lunch bunch and get out for a daily walk or watch your favorite TV show (especially *The Office,* which might make for parallel laughter).

3. *Establish "Sixty Minutes of Happiness" Gatherings:* Organize a happy hour with your coworkers once a week or once a month.

4. *Play Tell the Truth:* Gather trivia about the people on your team; send out a mapping-and-matching quiz and see who can correctly guess all of the matches.

5. *Picture This:* Photoshop pictures of your team onto a picture of superheroes or celebrities. Use these avatars in all your PowerPoint presentations.

6. *Get Cartoony:* Start a cartoon board and post some funnies for all to enjoy (*Dilbert,* anyone?).

7. *Showcase Your Kids:* Create a "Look at what my kid made!" or "Could you imagine my kid did this?" mural for employees to share their kids' creations and peccadillos.

8. *Learn a New Language:* If you work internationally, learn a few words and phrases of a language of one of your clients; surprise them with it in your next meeting.

9. *Learn More English:* Pick a word of the day or week, make sure it's obscure and esoteric, and ask everyone to create a funny sentence using it.

10. *Be Creative:* Brainstorm your own unique way of bringing humor to work. It's worth the added effort.

A SPECIAL NOTE ABOUT REMOTE WORKERS

Note that many of these exercises work just as well for a remote work-force. For remote teams, you can always start off with an icebreaker or a fun poll, use visuals to spice up your presentation, or add a gamification element to turn regular meetings into an interactive activity. The *Tell the Truth* game above works exceptionally well for remote teams that may have little opportunity to meet in person but who need to get to know one another more personally.

In fact, a culture of fun should not be limited only to special-activity time—it should influence every part of remote work. Presentations and meetings are great opportunities for you to add a little entertainment value to keep your team engaged. In an increasingly distributed workforce, virtual teambuilding activities have become an important measure for cultivating camaraderie and boosting motivation among remote employees. And with remote work here to stay, managing the needs of a remote team is basically equal to managing the needs of the future workplace.

PART
2

BETTER COMMUNICATION LEADS TO BETTER MANAGEMENT

MASTER THE ART OF ENGAGED LISTENING

Engaged listening is intended to describe how we relate with others in the workplace. How many times do managers complain of team members who aren't listening and just aren't fully on board? How many times do staff members complain of managers who appear to lack empathy or concern for the challenges they face? In fact, if you'd ever like a look behind the HR curtain to see what employees generally think of their managers' listening skills, pull aggregate data from your company's exit interviews. You'll likely get a striking dose of reality in realizing that listening gets significantly lower scores than you might otherwise imagine when departing employees are free to share their real insights into their supervisors' listening skills and engagement.

As the old saying goes, "If God intended us to talk more than listen, he would have given us two mouths and one ear." Said another way, "We have two ears and one mouth so that we can listen twice as much as we speak." Why is it that listening remains a constant challenge in the workplace on both the management and staff side of the equation? More precisely, why is it said that listening is the most important skill in communication?

Effective listening is the common term that describes the skill of actively absorbing information given to you by a speaker, showing that you are attentive and interested in turn, and providing feedback to the speaker so that he or she knows the message was received. Even more significant than effective listening is *engaged* listening, in which listeners hear with their heart in addition to their ears. What does that mean? It means that to be a truly engaged listener, you have to come from respect, from caring, and from empathy so that you lean into conversations and truly attempt to understand the other person's point of view.

The three most common types of listening in the business world are:

■ Informational listening (listening to learn)
■ Critical listening (listening to evaluate and analyze)
■ Empathetic listening (listening to understand feeling and emotion)

The first two types are what people typically think of when engaging in listening activities at work. It's where managers often go in their minds when they feel that team members aren't stepping up and mastering the material or performing at an acceptable level.

The third type, however, is your most critical issue as a leader. *Empathy* is the heart and soul of good listening. Listening to absorb and appreciate feelings and reactions is a critical part of emotional intelligence. This is a particular skill that, if honed and practiced over time, makes for great leaders, team builders, and career influencers.

The challenge for anyone in management, of course, is determining how to get there. Following are some typical recommendations from social scientists and communications experts for improving our ability to truly listen:

1. *Listen with your eyes.* Direct eye contact, at least in US culture, is a sign of respect and acknowledgment. Demonstrate your sincere interest in what the other person has to say by maintaining eye contact appropriately. Likewise, allow your body language to demonstrate that you're listening actively. Lean in. Avoid crossing your arms (typically considered defensive body language) and looking away from the speaker.

2. *Listen with your heart.* Interject occasionally to demonstrate that you are actively listening by paraphrasing with phrases like, "I see what you're saying." "I get it." "I understand so far." "I hear you." Likewise, you can paraphrase and acknowledge that you're truly hearing the other person's message by stating, "What I hear you saying is . . ." It might sound minor, but interestingly enough, the opposite happens all too often: the leader sits looking at his iPhone, the supervisor stares down at the floor, or the manager looks out the window in disgust and frustration. Whether you agree with what you're hearing or not, be open and transparent about truly trying to hear the other's perspective and point of view.

3. *Approach listening from the standpoint of observation rather than judgment.* You have every right to observe a situation, and you likewise have every right to your own point of view and perspective. Yet observation is different from judgment. Judgment adds a label—typically a negative one—that attaches ill motives and poor thinking to another person's actions. No one does anything wrong given their model of the world: listen openly, try to walk a mile in their shoes, and attempt to render objective observations. No matter what your message, it will be received more openly and likewise more respectfully if delivered with empathy and care.

4. *Count to two before you respond to someone else's statement.* Be careful not to interrupt—a cardinal sin that many earlier-career leaders tend to make. Each person has a point of view and the right to share it. This in no way lessens your ability to hold others accountable: it simply demonstrates that you genuinely care enough to hear the other's point of view before finalizing your recommended outcome or course of action. Likewise, don't proffer solutions at this stage. *Engaged listening* allows the other person to be heard first. Superimposing your answer onto their reality will likely not be appreciated nor serve as a teaching moment for your subordinate.

To experience empathy, you have to put yourself in the other person's place and allow yourself to feel what it is like to *be him or her* at that moment. This may not feel natural or particularly comfortable, but it is a generous and selfless thing to do. More important, it facilitates communication as nothing else does. In today's high-tech, high-speed, high-stress world, communication is more important than ever, yet we seem to devote less and less time to really listening to one another. Genuine listening has become a rare gift—the gift of time. It helps build relationships, solve problems, ensure understanding, resolve conflicts, and improve accuracy. Give the gift of your time and your heart when listening to others: all else will fall into place naturally.

8

THE ART OF SUCCESSFUL COMMUNICATION

SIMPLE GUIDELINES TO HELP YOUR MESSAGES SOAR

Communicating more effectively with your team starts with how you talk to people. The following guidelines are simple yet incredibly effective.

"PLEASE" AND "THANK YOU" STILL WORK!

As trite as this may sound, be sure and say "please" and "thank you" to your teams. You'd be surprised how often exiting employees make comments along the lines of this:

> People work so hard around here, yet we never hear a word of thanks. But when people make even just one little mistake, they'll be hearing from their boss like there's no tomorrow.

Along the same lines, follow the mantra of "What you want for yourself, give to another." That's not just spiritual guru talk—it's practical advice that injects greater humanity into the workplace, which in turn fosters a culture based on respect and more open communication. The executive coach asks, "Would you want to work for you?"

It might be harder for you to say yes to that question if you recognize yourself to be someone who has little patience for others, talks over them, or occasionally loses his temper and engages in public shaming sessions with subordinates.

GET TO KNOW YOUR EMPLOYEES ON A MORE PERSONAL LEVEL

Marcus Buckingham and Curt Coffman's bestselling book, *First, Break All the Rules: What the World's Greatest Managers Do Differently*, captured the Gallup organization's findings after studying eighty thousand managers and more than one million employees, and the results were clear: people join companies but leave managers. In other words, they join a company because they're excited about its reputation, accomplishments, mission, and similar factors, but they leave a few years later because of ongoing challenges they have with their immediate boss.

Gallup found that of all key retention factors (for example, company brand, benefits, and learning and development opportunities), nothing trumped employees' relationships with their immediate supervisors as the glue that bound them to the organization. The relationship should be personal—at least to some degree—so that team members know you care about their own personal interests and lives beyond work.

How do you accomplish this? Meet one-on-one with your direct reports and (occasionally) with your extended reports to find out how they're feeling about things. You might want to ask:

How are you doing, and how do you think we're doing overall as a department and team?

What could we be doing differently around here that would make a change in the results we're getting? If you could snap your fingers and change one thing about the way we do things, what would it be?

On a scale of one to ten, with ten being the highest, how engaged and motivated would you say you're feeling these days, and how would you grade the rest of the team?

On a scale of one to ten, with ten being the highest, how would you grade how well we work as a team? Why do you feel we're an [eight]? What could make us a nine or a ten?

Tell me about my communication style. And be honest—I really want to know. Do you get enough information to do your job well and keep yourself and your customers informed about upcoming changes? Likewise, do you feel that you have a voice and can make a difference in terms of how you do your job and how you get your work done?

What would you add or subtract to the way we communicate with one another as a team? Is there enough respect? Would you say we're good at teamwork? Do you trust that we have one another's backs and provide the right amount of internal support so that all team members can perform their very best work every day with minimal drama and full peace of mind?

Questions like these are endless, and you can customize them to address your own personal values or some of the challenges you may be facing as a team at any given point in time. What matters most is that you ask. Being a leader who cares doesn't mean that you have to know details about what's going on in your employees' personal lives (although some understanding of that is arguably very natural and healthy). It means you're taking the time to ask them about what matters most to them in the workplace and in their careers. Listen actively, seek their advice, and appreciate that the best suggestions will often come from those in the trenches who are closest to your customers' needs.

WHEN DELIVERING BAD NEWS, DON'T COME FROM ANGER

If you show that you're angry at your employees, their natural self-defense mechanisms will kick in, and the entire conversation will be off to a failed start. That's why yelling and shouting never work: at best, employees will obey out of fear or compliance, but fear and compliance will rarely get you to 100 percent in terms of effort and dedication. Instead, people will perform only to the minimum necessary to get the job done because they'll act either out of spite or out of resentment. What you're looking for is 110 percent on the effort scale—employees going above and beyond for the sake of their company, coworkers, or boss. It's that marginal difference that distinguishes strong, high-performing teams from those that struggle to satisfy minimum expectations.

Along the same lines, avoid using the word *why*—as in:

Why did you do that?

That question will typically trigger a self-defense response that focuses on deflecting criticism and avoiding blame. Instead, open the conversation with:

■ Share with me how that came about and what you were considering at the time.

- Share with me what you were considering when you made that decision.
- What were your thoughts at the time you decided to move in that direction?

By stating your question as an open invitation to provide more input, you'll typically get a much more candid and objective response that allows others to explain their side of the story (even if what they ultimately did was a mistake). An objective, nonjudgmental tone does wonders for keeping a conversation going in a healthy and constructive way.

TURN "YES . . . BUT" INTO "YES . . . AND" STATEMENTS

"Yes . . . but" responses often shut down a conversation right from the get-go. For example, instead of saying something like this:

Yes, I know we spoke about that, but you should have known . . .

Turn your statement into this:

Yes, I know we spoke about that, *and* I'm wondering what other choices were available to you at the time that you could have opted for . . .

So don't become a "Yes . . . but" communicator—an individual who potentially comes across as a naysayer, who appears to focus on the negative, and who tends to crush initiative and spontaneity. It's okay for you to spot weaknesses—that's a critical part of your role as a new manager and leader. But the way you bring those weaknesses to others' attention or help them realize the shortcomings in their reasoning will help you foster and nurture talent rather than shut it down.

SPEAK FROM GUILT MORE THAN ANGER

Here I'm not referring to old-fashioned guilt that stems from putting people down or otherwise shaming them into doing something. Instead, I'm looking at guilt as a natural human emotion that helps people look inward for solutions and come from a more selfless orientation where it's safe to feel vulnerable and assume partial responsibility for something gone wrong.

When it comes to expressing dissatisfaction with an employee's performance or conduct, coming more from guilt (or "awareness") rather than from anger typically garners much more favorable results. First, anger is an external emotion: if people feel angry, they're pointing their energy outward at someone or something else. They feel defensive and instinctively look to justify their actions by proving the other person wrong and themselves right. On the other hand, guilt, as a human emotion, helps people look inward for answers and, as such, helps people make themselves partially responsible for a problem so they can help resolve it in a more cooperative spirit.

For example, if you believe a subordinate was inappropriate or somewhat disrespectful during a staff meeting, you could raise the stakes by going toe-to-toe during the meeting in front of the rest of the team as follows:

I can't believe you used that tone of voice with me in front of the rest of the team. You report to me, and last I looked, the stripes on my shoulder are a bit higher than yours!

Although that may make you feel better for a moment as you let off steam, clearly it does little to help you understand what was really going on that led to the inappropriate comment or remark.

Instead, if you handle the matter quietly and in private, you'll arguably get a much more desirable response by stating something like this:

> Ashley, I'm not quite sure what happened in that meeting. We've always had a mutually respectful relationship, but it seemed to me like you needed to work out a lot of pent-up anger in there, and the fact that you did that in front of the rest of the team really *embarrassed* me.
>
> I respect you too much to call you out like that in front of others, and I wouldn't have expected you to act that way toward me, especially in front of the rest of the team. Can you understand why I might feel let down by your actions in there? It really hurt my feelings.

Said quietly and softly with a serious tone of voice, no drama was needed—no escalation, no threats, and no pulling rank—and your message will likely have a much stronger impact than had you escalated emotions by yelling. The typical employee response might be:

> Oh, I'm sorry, Paul, I didn't intend to embarrass you in any way, especially in front of the rest of the team. I apologize for my actions in there and promise that'll never happen again.

Enough said.

SPEAK OF "PERCEPTION" AND HOLD YOUR EMPLOYEES ACCOUNTABLE FOR THEIR OWN "PERCEPTION MANAGEMENT"

Finally, when delivering bad news, add the words "perception" or "perception management" to your vocabulary. Feelings aren't right or wrong—they just are what they are. The same goes for perception: you're entitled to your own perception, and sharing what things look like from your vantage point isn't right or wrong—it just is what it is.

For example, telling a member of your staff that he has a *bad attitude* will likely trigger all sorts of drama. Adults tend to get all weird when they're told they have an attitude problem, so let's approach it a different way:

> Michele, I think it's time that we sit down and address some concerns that have been on my mind for quite some time. Working with you can be challenging at times, and I'm guessing this isn't the first time you're hearing this. Let me share with you what things feel like from my vantage point as your supervisor.
>
> From a perception standpoint, you can come across as angry much of the time. I'm not sure what triggers hostility on your part or what I may be doing in terms of pushing some sort of hot button when I'm working with you, but your responses with me tend to be aggressive and confrontational. Truth be told, I tend to avoid you at times because I'm not sure what kind of response I'm going to get.
>
> Likewise, your mood fluctuates often, and I've heard from others that "you never know what kind of response you're going to get from Michele because it depends which way the wind is blowing." That's been my experience as well on a number of occasions.
>
> I'll make a commitment to you now that I won't walk on eggshells around you anymore or avoid partnering with you. I shouldn't have to, and neither should anyone else. Regardless of your reality or however you've been justifying your behavior in your mind up to now, I'll simply not accept irrational or moody behavior from this point forward. You've got a significant perception problem on your hands, and from now on, I'm holding you fully accountable for your own perception management. If you're not successful managing how you come across to others or in any way make it difficult for people to work with

you, then my response will be in writing in the form of formal progressive discipline. And depending on the nature of the complaint and who informs me of it, I'll arguably be starting the corrective action at either the written or the final written warning stage.

If you feel you can't or won't reinvent yourself in terms of how you're coming across to others and to me, then you may want to rethink remaining with this organization. You've been here for eighteen years, which I respect, but in my last three months since joining the firm, you've shown me what feels like resistance at every turn. You come across to me as if I'm interrupting you or bothering you when I ask for your help or ask you a simple question. I feel that you don't have my back, are leaving me flying blind, and are otherwise not supportive of my success.

If you're willing to turn a new leaf and reinvent your relationship with me and with others, then I'm fully on board and will support you in any way I can. If you'd like access to resources like our employee assistance program (EAP) or additional training on dealing with conflict in the workplace, I'll be happy to provide them. But if you're not willing to make that commitment to me, to the organization, and to yourself, then I'd ask you to please not put me in a situation where I need to reach out to HR to initiate corrective action that could ultimately lead to your termination. You deserve better as a long-term employee, but I deserve better as your supervisor as well. What are your thoughts?

Yes, that's a tough conversation, but you'll have created a clear verbal record of your impressions and your expectations, and that's a healthy place to start. It's now up to the employee to measure herself by how others view and describe her and to remain open to reestablishing her relationship with her boss, coworkers, and clients.

9

THREE STEPS TO GREAT STAFF MEETINGS

Improving communication with your staff starts with healthy group dialogue, and a regular, ongoing, and predictable forum to voice new ideas and safely suggest alternative ways of doing things will always be your best place to start. No matter how strong your relationships with particular individuals on your team or how long you've all been working together, the group dynamic takes on a life of its own during the weekly staff meeting. It, more than just about anything, gives you an opportunity to open the lines of communication with your team, demonstrate recognition for a job well done, and place individual contributors into rotational leadership roles. There are three basic steps to a successful staff meeting.

First, invite all of your subordinates to discuss what's going on in their worlds. Brief updates and overviews of achievements, roadblocks, and opportunities to reinvent the workflow are hallmarks of healthy group get-togethers. It's not only important for individuals to talk about themselves, however; it's also critical that all members of the staff hear what their peers are doing. Too many times, employees dig proverbial foxholes for themselves and develop an entitlement mentality in which they believe they're doing all the work. Once they hear what everyone else is working on, they tend to develop a greater appreciation for their peers' contributions. Their sense of entitlement will typically diminish as a result.

Second, focus on what you, as a group, could have done differently in the past week to make the company a better place. After all, that's what work is all about. We're hired to increase revenues, decrease expenses, and save time. Any lost opportunities to impact the company's bottom line in one of those three ways should be discussed, studied, and revisited in this postmortem exercise. Ask the group this question:

What could we have done differently?

This question mirrors what's going on in your group at any given time. It also allows for a healthy dose of self-critical insight and makes it safe to learn from past mistakes.

Third, introduce constructive criticism into the decision-making process. Specifically, ask:

What do we need to be doing differently going forward as a team?

What can I do to provide greater structure, support, and direction?

What do you see as our biggest challenge this week?

The best ideas will always come from the people on the front line. The frustration that many employees share with HR during employee opinion surveys or exit interviews is that they didn't feel that their ideas mattered or that managers and senior leaders were listening. These employees went through the motions day in and day out but felt they had no real impact or influence over their working environment. This simple invitation satisfies the basic need to be heard and to make a positive difference.

Where do these weekly staff meetings lead? You'll soon see the following benefits:

- First and foremost, you'll strengthen the overall bond and cohesiveness of the work unit when you encourage communication, recognition, and trust.
- Second, by giving your people more "face time" with you, the boss, and with one another, a greater spirit of camaraderie will develop.
- Third, these meetings tend to expand from the micro view of work assignments and project updates to the more macro level of organizational impact.
- All in all, your investment in a group meeting like this will likely end up being the most important hour of the week in terms of enhancing productivity and teamwork.

In fact, one of the surest signs of a dysfunctional group is that it doesn't hold regular staff meetings. The "we give one another informal feedback all the time" excuse tends to be a cop-out in all but the most trusted situations in which team members have been working together for a long time and work independently. Instead, your antennae should go up when you hear something like this:

Staff meetings aren't necessary because we all know what everyone is working on.

If staffers aren't talking collectively as a group on a regular basis, it's more often a sign that people are working in silos and that cliques exist, which creates a more restricted and divided working environment.

If this is the case in your group or in a team that you're now responsible for overseeing, it could be fairly simple to inject a staff meeting structure into the workweek—no matter how busy everyone's schedule is or how little time they have to take the focus off their work. You can instruct your team as follows and, depending on what your team is responsible for, focus your team efforts on the critical issues at hand. Try something like this:

> Everyone, I called this meeting to let you know that I want to begin holding formal weekly team meetings. I think there's a lot of value in that sort of group interaction because I want you all to have an opportunity to share with your peers what priorities you're working on, what challenges and roadblocks you may be facing, and how the rest of us could help you in terms of additional support or resources. I also think it'll give us a chance to share and celebrate successes, which is something we don't do enough of. Here are my recommendations:
>
> First, be prepared to give an overview of the top three projects or assignments you're working on in terms of progress, deliverables, and timelines. If you suspect you may have any challenges meeting deadlines, this is the place for us to find out so that we can all make ourselves part of the solution.
>
> Second, I'd like you to address the biggest programs or projects you're working on that week—David, in your case, that would be metrics development; Juanita, in your case, that might be employee communications in light of the recent employee opinion survey that we conducted; Ebony, I'd ask you to share your insights into the mentoring relationship you have with the two recent new hires and how that's helped them assimilate into our team more successfully.
>
> Finally, I'll ask you all to discuss what we could be doing differently as a team and how I could support you further by removing roadblocks and facilitating progress toward the goals you're working on.

This will also give us opportunities to rotate staff meeting leadership. After the first month of meetings that I'll lead, I'll ask each of you to volunteer to lead these meetings and be responsible for any follow-up items. Let's launch this, assume good intentions, and give it our all. I think this could be a game changer in terms of our team's productivity, and more important, I think this could be a lot of fun. I'm looking forward to your contributions, so let's tee up the first meeting for this Thursday at eight thirty.

Resist the temptation to back-burner weekly staff meetings, no matter how much pushback you get from your staffers. This is one of those situations where they might not know what's best for them; but formalizing the lines of communication and giving yourself multiple opportunities to reset expectations and hear about feedback in real time is an advantage and an opportunity that you won't want to do without.

10

FACILITATING INFORMATION SHARING

QUARTERLY ACHIEVEMENT CALENDARS

Getting your team on the same page is easier to do with the help of an Excel spreadsheet or SharePoint and a departmental shared drive. Everyone on the team should have equal access to this spreadsheet that tracks key projects, developments, upcoming events, and completion notes. With a tool like this in hand, little will fall through the cracks, information about what people are doing is universally visible, achievements can be easily codified for everyone to see, and accomplishments can be celebrated.

This one document unifies your group's efforts and allays any concerns individual workers sometimes fall victim to when they say, "I'm the only one who does any work around here, and no one else seems to do nearly as much as I do." Next, it ties nicely to quarterly goal assignments, and it keeps your team focused on the end goal at all times, which helps them prioritize their workload and allocate resources efficiently. Ask them all to focus on quantifying the results in terms of either increased revenue, decreased costs, or saved time. They could do that in the forms of dollars and cents or percentages.

And voilà! You have a team that's fully informed and on top of what's going on, who's working on what, how many projects are pending versus closed, and how to quantify their results in terms of dollars or percentages. That's just the material they need as employees to add bullets to their resumes and self-evaluation forms when holding performance discussions with you, their manager, every three months. You might also create a desktop shortcut on your boss's desk so that he or she is aware of your group's focus areas and quarterly and year-to-date achievements.

Talk about informed leadership, transparent communication, and efficient time management! Most important, this helps you spend your time strategically in terms of gaining the benefit of a broad overview of all the moving parts. This particular step of creating a performance-driven philosophy is fairly simple to implement and a key benefit to any frontline leader, department, or division head. It could also be a game changer for individuals on your team because internal competition for garnering hard-core achievements places peer pressure on those who might otherwise be "performing to the minimums."

Scorecards and dashboards are fun and creative to develop and can also be a creative exercise in which everyone participates and contributes. Just be sure that you're grading your team and sharing results no less than quarterly. That's the minimum interval for keeping everyone fully engaged and on top of things.

QUARTERLY ACHIEVEMENT CALENDAR STRUCTURE

A simple template that staff members will be responsible for updating weekly might be structured as follows:

STAFF MEMBER	
PROJECT TITLE	
PRIORITY (A, B, C)	
DATE BEGUN	
KEY STAKEHOLDERS	
CURRENT STATUS / ADJUSTMENTS NEEDED	
PROJECTED COMPLETION DATE	
ACTUAL COMPLETION DATE	
NOTES	

11

SKIP-LEVEL MEETINGS HELP MANAGERS COMMUNICATE WITH EMPLOYEES WHO AREN'T DIRECT REPORTS

Many companies struggle occasionally with a particular department that wrestles with chronic underperformance and stability challenges. Yet few senior leaders take the time to conduct "skip-level" meetings, where they have an opportunity to bypass their midlevel managers and speak directly with members of their extended (non-managerial) teams.

For example, if a corporate vice president wishes to speak with the team members of a director on that team, then the VP can hold one-on-one meetings with the manager and supervisor and small group meetings with the rest of the team—analysts, coordinators, administrative assistants, and the like. It's best to be fully transparent about this, and yes, staff members may feel a bit uncomfortable sharing their feedback with their boss's boss. But these meetings are healthy and should be ongoing to ensure full transparency and access to senior management. You'll want to always be prepared for requests from your boss or your boss's boss to speak with your team directly.

Holding skip-level meetings is a management best practice that occurs on a regular basis in many high-performing organizations. In other situations, skip-level meetings only tend to occur where there is a problem: for example, when ongoing performance and conduct challenges weigh negatively on team performance or where turnover is rampant. Just remember that it's healthy for your immediate supervisor or department head to want to speak with your team without you being present. More often than not, it's simply a formal way for senior leaders to understand how middle management is handling things. But it's likewise true that skip-level meetings may occur more frequently when specific challenges arise. What should you expect and how can you prepare your teams for skip-level meetings?

First, encourage your manager and your manager's manager to engage directly with your team in skip-level meetings. Nothing speaks confidence and transparency more than a manager inviting senior leaders to do so. It can be a great opportunity for the team to get to know your boss more personally and an excellent learning opportunity for you in terms of your own career growth and development. In doing so, you also have a greater degree of control over the process. For example, you can speak with your immediate supervisor and find out what's typically discussed in such meetings. This way, you can build your communication plan with your team around the key focus areas that are important to your boss.

Second, it's a healthy leadership exercise for you to understand how skip-level meetings are handled at the senior management level. Yes, even senior executives have to be trained, so here's a behind-the-scenes look at how senior leaders are trained to conduct skip-level meetings.

BE SPECIFIC

Senior leaders typically open skip-level meetings by being specific and providing as many details as possible about the feedback they've received, especially if it's problematic. For example, their group opener might sound like this:

As you're aware, I decided to conduct skip-level meetings in order to hear directly from the staff members of those who report to me. The purpose of skip-level meetings with your team and the teams of my other direct reports is to gauge the overall culture and level of employee satisfaction and engagement on our team. Therefore, I wanted to ask you all:

How would you grade our senior leadership team in terms of communication and our ability to listen to and address employees' concerns?

How would you grade departmental leadership in terms of communication, teambuilding, respect, and inclusiveness?

On a scale of one to ten, how well would you say you function as a team (with ten being highest)? Why are you an [eight]? What would make you a ten?

Do you feel you can do your best work every day? In other words, do you feel like leadership has your back and supports you? What would you recommend we do differently?

If you could change one thing about the way things operate around here, what would your number one recommendation be?

You get the idea. Senior leaders who care about people often take the opportunity to speak directly with the individual contributors who make the department hum. To do so fairly and objectively, however, they have to remove the immediate group or team leader.

How do you prepare for a skip-level meeting that may come your way? First, speak with your boss about the critical drivers of team success. What's critical to her and how can you make that a mantra of your own (assuming you agree with it)? Ask for specific examples of what it looks like when done correctly versus incorrectly. Are there any land mines you should be aware of? Are there any other leaders in the organization who do this particularly well that you can emulate or speak with?

Second, make these values part of the talking points you share with your teams during weekly staff meetings and quarterly one-on-one reviews. Trying to force this at the last minute doesn't work well: it will feel insincere at best and manipulative at worst. Make speaking about values and experiences at your organization an occasional talking point. If someone starts in with, "This company *never* pays enough; it *always* gives in to the squeaky wheel, and nothing's going to ever change," that gives you a chance to exercise wisdom and leadership by setting the record straight. Specifically, you can advise your team to stay away from *always* and *never* sentences because they're typically exaggerated and rarely true. That being said, you have an opportunity to hear your employees' gripes in a safe environment, which you can then proactively share with your immediate supervisor in order to formulate an appropriate response.

Just be careful not to sweep employees' concerns under the rug. If you're going to ask, you have to be willing to do something about it. That something typically starts with bringing the matter to your boss for an initial level of resolution. At their best, skip-level meetings look to unearth concerns or roadblocks that may be hampering performance, so accept them in the positive light they're intended.

On the other hand, if your boss is stepping in because of ongoing problems with the team, try to get ahead of that and enlist your boss's support proactively so that she's on your side from the outset. Skip-level meetings are only intended to help—not catch anyone "being bad." But it would be naïve to assume they'll never happen to you since they're fairly common at many organizations. Make this part of your strategic communication and teambuilding plan from the start. You'll hone your proactive leadership skills and become more confident in welcoming such interventions in the future.

CONFRONTATION IS A NECESSARY PART OF COMMUNICATION

No one wants to confront others at work if they can possibly avoid it. (In fact, if they do want to, they've probably got other, more serious problems on their hands!) But we have to focus on human nature to understand why communication can be so difficult and challenging. People tend to shy away from discussing uncomfortable issues and prefer to take a "let's wait and see if it fixes itself" approach whenever possible. Sometimes, things do end up straightening themselves out without any form of external intervention, but most of us would agree that's more the exception than the rule.

In reality, this natural trend toward avoidance shows itself in many untoward ways in the workplace:

- An unwillingness to address minor impediments verbally before they become larger-scale roadblocks
- A reluctance to issue formal corrective action for fear of upsetting or demotivating an employee
- Grade inflation on the annual performance review so as to avoid offending or disappointing the recipient with critical feedback that was likely long overdue

These common land mines may plague us throughout our career if we don't acknowledge them and determine a strategy for communicating effectively through them, and the time to hone that skill—especially for new managers—is right now.

Here's a hint: this isn't as hard as it seems! Remember, it's not what you say but how you say it that counts. Let's focus on building the *how* in the equation so that it actually becomes easier to deliver challenging news and hold people accountable to higher expectations.

First, we have to spend a few minutes understanding how we're naturally wired. Whether it's via our quirky individual personalities or millennia of practice, adults have certain hang-ups about communication. Understanding where we come from is therefore important because it can shed light on where we're going. More specifically, knowing that any and all of these quagmires face us as leaders at different times and to differing degrees, it's important that we explore and understand that certain adult behaviors are actually built into us from childhood and have to be overcome to attain recognition as a great communicator.

The easiest way for us to view communication challenges in the workplace in a more common context can be seen in its parallelism to parenting. For the sake of this argument, let's assume that Dad is taking care of the kids at home while Mom is out working. If little Nina and Sam are driving Dad crazy because they just won't get along with one another, how does Dad stop the annoying behavior, raise behavioral expectations, and stop the roller-coaster ride so that the problem doesn't keep popping up?

Let's look at three models of parenting that reveal the choices at hand very clearly. In each scenario, let's assume that the kids are at it again and Dad is about to go ballistic and is at the end of his rope. See which model sounds most familiar to you in terms of your own upbringing:

Model 1: Dad shouts, "Kids, you're driving me crazy! Go out and play and when you come back, I don't expect to hear any more bickering!"

Okay, not an uncommon response; the core logic is that the problem will fix itself once the kids are otherwise distracted. But if this approach does work, it's usually not for very long, as the frustrated father realizes once the kids are back in the house and the bickering picks up where it left off.

Model 2: Dad shouts, "Kids, you're driving me crazy! If you don't knock it off, you're both going to be in so much trouble when your mother gets home."

Again, a fairly common approach, although Dad just totally minimized his role and gave total power over to Mom, who isn't even home and doesn't know there's a problem. The kids typically figure out pretty quickly that Dad's threats are pretty hollow, he'll forget all about it by the time Mom gets home, and they're at liberty to pick up the fight anytime and anywhere they want because they know that Dad isn't going to do anything about it other than make some hollow threats about Mom's wrath (which never materializes).

Model 3: Dad shouts, "Kids, you're driving me crazy! Come in here right now and close the door behind you. We're going to talk about what's going on because I expect more of both of you."

Ah, an interesting twist. Once the kids sit down, Dad calmly opens the discussion by saying, "Nina, I want you to say something nice about your brother." (Nina rolls her eyeballs and begrudgingly says, "You've got pretty eyes, Sam.") Dad then turns to Sam and says, "Sammy, say something nice about your sister Nina." (Sam harrumphs and says, "I really like the painting you made me this morning.")

Okay, now we're getting somewhere: we set the tone of the "intervention" to be positive and constructive. Now that the kids have settled down a bit and gained some perspective (although reluctantly) on the situation, they're prepared to discuss why the other is bugging them. At the conclusion of their explanations, Dad then has the opportunity to reset expectations in a calm voice and reassure them that in this household, a certain level of behavior is expected of the children and it's his job to ensure that they don't forget that. The kids can then give each other a hug, smile, and move on to other things.

Notice the paradigm shift in model 3: there's no avoiding (model 1) and no deflecting (model 2). The wisdom that the father shows in model 3 is that he's in total control, he's there to remind the kids of the expectations that he has of them, and he's there to support them both through an uncomfortable set of circumstances.

But there's a critical difference between this scenario with Dad and the kids and what you'll typically face in the workplace: siblings can sit down cold in the midst of an argument and settle their dispute amicably. Not so with adults—they can't be brought into your office cold and asked to sit down and fix a problem right on the spot. Adults aren't wired that way: sibling kids can do it because they've grown up together and know and trust one another instinctively, while adults in the workplace don't have enough trust to solve the "what" of the problem as well as the "how" of the solution all in one sitting.

Instead, adult coworkers typically need to participate in separate meetings (preferably with a night of sleep between both meetings) to first determine the "what" (that is, the facts and allegations) and then—after a good night's sleep—to work on the "how" (the solution and their commitment to avoiding such behaviors again in the future). So, if you bring two warring parties cold into your office to end an ongoing dispute and order them to "knock it off," expect a whole lot of drama and tension. Adults are too afraid of being attacked (again, the "what" of the issue and the ensuing allegations) and typically will not listen openly. Instead, they'll be prepared to jump on the other person as soon as something "wrong" is said, leading to rolling eyeballs, glares, sarcastic laughter, and the like. (Remember the best defense is a preemptive offense!)

So don't expect warring parties to fix the "what" and "how" in one sitting: they're simply too socialized and not trusting enough at this point in their social development to assume good intentions and make themselves vulnerable. But this is a way for you, as their manager, to make it relatively safe to address their concerns openly and even assume partial responsibility for the problem at hand. As in most things in life, it's all in the setup.

THE STRUCTURE OF CONFRONTIVE CONFRONTATION:
When Two Employees Continuously Clash with One Another

Step 1

Meet with Employee A and hear his side of the story. Share with him that you want to listen to and take notes of everything he has to say in terms of the problems he's experiencing with Employee B. However, inform him at the outset of the meeting that everything he shares with you in good faith will be presented to Employee B after the meeting. Same goes for when he meets with Employee B to hear her side of the story: he'll take copious notes and truly listen to her side of the story, but everything she shares with him will be communicated to you after that meeting. This way, by the end of the day, both employees will know the nature of the other's concerns (i.e., the "what" of it all).

Step 2

Schedule a follow-up meeting with Employee A and Employee B the next morning to discuss the "how" of fixing the problems that exist on both sides. Remember, the genie was let out of the bottle the day before where both employees had an opportunity to share their concerns with you, the manager and objective arbiter of the dispute. Both also heard their coworker's account of what's occurring that's aggravating and frustrating them. With this "what" now behind you and a night to sleep on it, the group meeting the next morning can begin with the following ground rules:

Step 3

1. You've both had an opportunity to share your concerns with me about the other.

2. I've listened carefully to you both, specifically regarding the complaints you had about one another. I likewise shared with you both what the other person's concerns were.

3. Our goal in this morning's meeting is to move beyond the "what" of the problem and focus on the "how" of the solution. How can you alter your own behaviors knowing what you now know to elicit a different response from the other person going forward? What are you each willing to do differently now that you've heard the other person's concerns?

4. Just remember that there is no attacking or defending allowed in this meeting. You both have valid points about the problem, but that's behind us—yesterday's news, so to speak. For today, don't hold anything back but soothe your words with kindness, providing feedback in a constructive manner. Then focus on what you're willing to do differently now that you've walked a mile in the other person's shoes. What are you willing to do

from a selfless leadership standpoint to elicit a different response from the other person going forward?

Said softly and empathetically, this meeting structure removes participants' feelings of having to defend themselves from prior events and simply focus on future solutions. When there's no need to defend, there's little reason to attack. And with you there guiding them through their differences and their future commitments, you will most likely experience the positive outcome you were hoping for.

No, you're not expecting them to become best friends outside of work, but you'll have the opportunity to reset your expectations in terms of how they treat and respect one another. You might even throw in that this is a once-in-a-career benefit and that if an eruption occurs again, your only recourse will likely be in the form a documented written warning for both. That healthy caveat will let "the kids" know that you're no longer avoiding this, you're not waiting for anyone else to fix it, and you're holding them both fully accountable for their behavior toward one another going forward. There's nothing like simple, direct communication of expectations when it comes to setting employees up to hold themselves fully accountable for meeting company conduct standards.

TOUGH CONVERSATIONS

YOUR MORAL OBLIGATION TO
CONFRONT CONSTRUCTIVELY

Effectively managing performance can help avoid termination of employees and boost productivity at all levels of your organization. After all, the goal of any performance management system is to empower, reward, motivate, and align your team. It's that last verb—*align*—that requires constructive management interventions from time to time. So, if you dread having difficult conversations with staff members when there's a performance or conduct problem at hand, you're not alone. But it's still a critical part of your job as a frontline leader and manager.

The path of least resistance is avoidance, and managers often opt to allow problem issues to fix themselves rather than intercede and address them head-on. That's not an unreasonable approach: with workloads so demanding, time so limited, and workers feeling overwhelmed and burned out these days, sidestepping confrontational issues may make sense at first. But when insidious behaviors begin to pepper the workplace and affect other members of the team, it becomes time to engage. After all, every manager-employee relationship is a partnership, and true partnerships thrive on trust, respect, and transparency. Best advice: keep your immediate boss and human resources in the loop before you venture down these paths, because you always want to line up your resources in advance and ensure there are no surprises down the road.

IMPORTANT RULES OF THE GAME

Remember what we all learned in the third grade: *it's not what you say but how you say it that counts.* This simple truth is as valuable today as it was when you first learned it: people will respond more favorably to even the harshest criticism if it's shared with their best interests in mind. "Why did you do that?" "What were you thinking?" and similar approaches only prompt defensive reactions in others, so avoid triggering tempers by coming from the wisdom of "What's so" rather than from "So what." In other words, you have every right to observe what's so, you're entitled to your own objective vantage point, and your feelings are valid in and of themselves. But observing and judging are two vastly different things, so leave the judgmental "so what" piece behind, whenever possible, especially by avoiding the *why* construct, which makes people feel like they have to justify their actions and go on the defensive.

While the adage may be true that it's not what you say but how you say it, *what you say* is critically important as well. Well-meaning supervisors have experienced unintended consequences by stepping on land mines they didn't see. For example, "sexual harassment" is a legal conclusion. It's fine to say to someone that you "failed to create a friendly and inclusive work environment," "your actions indicate that you *may have violated* Policy XYZ on antiharassment and discrimination," and other "specifically vague" phrases. But don't state to an employee that he "sexually harassed" someone else. And by all means, don't codify that in writing in the form of progressive disciplinary action. Subpoenas can pull these documents magically from an employee's personnel file months or years later, and your codified "legal conclusion" that harassment occurred can go a long way in strengthening a plaintiff attorney's case against your company.

Finally, *perception is reality until proven otherwise.* As mentioned elsewhere in this book series, all employees are responsible for their own "perception management." We tend to judge others by their actions and ourselves by our intentions. It's important to raise awareness about this critical responsibility of remaining accountable for the perception you create in others; otherwise, it gets too easy to point fingers and blame elsewhere and refuse to assume partial responsibility for the problem yourself.

ADDRESSING MINOR PROBLEMS BEFORE THEY BECOME MAJOR IMPEDIMENTS

One of the most common challenges facing managers is dealing with employee attitude problems. If an entitlement mentality evidenced by rolling eyeballs, sighs, and antagonistic body language drives you crazy, you're not alone. Still, trying to stop such "silent" behaviors is difficult because it's so easily denied by employees.

More often than not, supervisors tend to avoid confrontation associated with employees who "cop a 'tude" because the allegation can be so easily denied. After all, as a manager, you don't want to come across as too touchy or overly sensitive. Still, the feelings of resentment linger and all too often result in buried frustration that erupts in a public shouting match when some proverbial "last straw" is broken on the camel's back, and by then the situation is out of control.

When attempting to eradicate this all-too-common problem, tell the person in private how you perceive her actions and how she makes you feel. Feelings aren't right or wrong: they just are. Ask for her help in solving the *perception* problem that exists and make a mutual commitment to understand that person's side of the story and better the situation.

Further, whenever you deal with what you perceive to be an "attitude" problem, be sure to avoid the word *attitude*. It's simply too subjective and inflammatory a word and typically escalates disagreement by fostering feelings of resentment and anger. As a matter of fact, courts have interpreted "attitude problems" as mere differences of opinion or personality conflicts. It is therefore critical that you avoid that specific term in any of your disciplinary documentation. Only behaviors and actions that can be observed and documented may be presented as evidence in court. Therefore, refer to "conduct" or "behavior" when addressing the issue of unacceptable "attitude."

Likewise, add "career coaching" language to your discussion so the employee perceives your interaction as constructive and potentially beneficial:

> Lucas, I'm sharing this with you because I don't want to see this hold you back in any way. You might not even be aware of it, but I wouldn't be doing you a service as your supervisor if I didn't bring this to your attention. And I'm not sharing this only for the benefit of your co-workers here at XYZ Company: this is meant to be professional advice for the rest of your career. Fix this now while you've got me in your corner so you'll know how to address this if it ever pops up again.

GAINING A VERBAL COMMITMENT

When attempting to fix a problem that exists with one of your staff members, look to gain the appropriate commitment as follows:

> Noah, I need your help. You know they say that perception is reality until proven otherwise. I feel like you're either angry with me or upset

with the rest of the group. I may be off in my assumption, but I think it's fair to say you likely have a *perception problem* on your hands. I don't know if anything's bothering you or if you feel that I can be more supportive of you in any way, but please let me know if that's the case. Otherwise, though, understand that *you make me feel* embarrassed in front of other members of the staff when you roll your eyes upward and sigh, "Okay, I'll get it done!" Do you feel it's inappropriate for me to ask you to complete your work on time? Should I even have to follow up with you regarding project completion deadlines, or should it be your responsibility to keep me abreast of that status of your projects? *How would you feel if* you were the supervisor and one of your staff members responded that way to you in front of others?

Note that the best remedy for curing this kind of problem is by helping the employee view the situation through a different lens—namely, yours. Remember that the normal reaction for most of us is to respond with anger. But anger is external—it forces people to look beyond themselves for fault. That's why employees typically blame others when they're the recipients of a manager's attacks. Guilt, in its healthiest form, works better than anger under these circumstances because it raises awareness and helps the individual look inward for a solution, which is all that's typically needed to fix something once and for all.

End your meeting by asking:

Noah, can you make a commitment to me that you'll assume full responsibility going forward for the perceptions you create, meaning your words and your silent behavior? [*Yes.*]

Great. I'd also like a commitment from you that this will be the last time we'll have to discuss this. Is that a fair request on my part, and can you make that commitment to me as well? [*Yes.*]

And with that verbal commitment, you'll have created an important record going forward should further disciplinary action become necessary.

Remember, conduct infractions are sometimes the most difficult to quantify but the most detrimental to department morale. Whenever you feel like disrespectful, belligerent employees are holding you hostage, put the brakes on their actions without escalating emotions. Simply demonstrate respect for your subordinates by handling matters privately behind closed doors with a verbal coaching session. It is typically wise to document the date and nature of the conversation in your notes should you need to refer to this verbal commitment at some point in the future. Only such a consistent approach will put a stop to aggravating and disrespectful behavior meant to challenge and undermine your managerial authority.

ENCOURAGING SOMEONE TO LEAVE YOUR COMPANY BY RESIGNING

WHEN IT'S RIGHT FOR YOU AND RIGHT FOR THEM

Sometimes it becomes necessary to convince employees to leave your company. Why? Because employees who are experiencing serious performance or conduct problems will often stay "on principle"—in other words, they'll rationalize that they'll stay till *they're* good and ready to leave. "No one's forcing me out of my job until I'm ready to go—especially not that boss of mine!" goes the logic of the disenfranchised and victimized worker.

Unfortunately, the negative impact that these employees have on their coworkers is often underestimated. The results can be very problematic: workers' comp stress claims and leaves of absence, union grievances, or wrongful termination lawsuits await when embattled workers somehow see themselves as standing up to mean and nasty employers. Reciprocally, months or years of feeling unappreciated and having their egos and self-esteem bashed await the fellow employees. So your best solution from an employee-relations standpoint is to broker a peace in which one party may walk out of the working relationship with dignity and respect intact.

PROCEED WITH CAUTION!

Some caveats from the outset: You must ensure that your company's HR team is fully on board with an approach like this before you launch into it. Ditto for your senior leadership team: your immediate boss and the department head must fully approve discussions like this before they occur. In fact, it's always a smart idea to involve your company (or an outside employment defense) attorney before proceeding with these types of employee interventions.

First, meetings such as this require a third-party mediator (typically HR or a senior member of management); if immediate supervisors who are part of the problematic interpersonal relationship with disenfranchised employees attempt to "talk them into" leaving their job, those supervisors' efforts may be seen as insincere or self-serving at best. Second, bear in mind that whatever is shared with the employee in meetings like this may take on a different meaning six months down the road when the company is being sued for "constructive discharge."

A *constructive discharge claim* is similar to wrongful discharge; however, in the constructive discharge case, the employee resigns and is not terminated by the company. Still, a plaintiff attorney will typically argue that the conditions were so intolerable at work that any reasonable person would have resigned under similar circumstances. (Per the US Supreme Court's interpretation of the constructive discharge doctrine, the key question is, did working conditions become so intolerable that a reasonable person in the employee's position would have felt compelled to resign?) Consequently, the plaintiff attorney will argue, "My client was forced into resigning her position, and the company had no right to create such a hostile working environment. Her supervisor told her that she wasn't wanted there anymore and had no future with the company! He demeaned her and embarrassed her publicly on multiple occasions. Telling her that after three years of dedicated service and one full year of isolating her from the rest of the team, denying her a raise, withholding training, and holding her to a higher standard than everyone else was just too much. She had to quit, but it was *their* fault."

We all know that when it comes to job performance problems, both sides are often in total disagreement about the situation. Managers argue that the problematic employee is disrespectful, noncommunicative, and does not hold herself accountable for her own actions. As a result, managers complain, "I delegate as little to her as I can. Instead, I do the work myself or give it to the other members of the team. My other staff members resent that she doesn't do her own share of the work, and they're tired of my cutting a wide swath around this employee for fear of upsetting her or making matters worse."

The disenfranchised employee in this same scenario will argue, almost as if holding up a mirror, "Are you kidding? My boss shows me no respect, she never makes me feel like part of the team, and she constantly holds me to a higher standard than everyone else. I'm never in the communication loop, and I'm never told when I do something right—only when I do something wrong. I'm sick and tired of being worked so hard and treated so unfairly!"

Who's right and who's wrong in these situations? Both sides. Employees too often take the easy road out and justify their irresponsible behavior by arguing favoritism and blaming their bosses for their own unhappiness. Managers, however, have clearly failed in their responsibility of creating a working environment where employees can motivate themselves and make a positive contribution to the department's goals. In essence, if the working relationship has deteriorated to this point, both the manager and worker have failed. Sometimes, however, trying to fix these problems just becomes an ongoing battle of wills where little good results.

THIRD-PARTY INTERMEDIARIES TO THE RESCUE

Human resources or senior management typically functions as this third-party mediator that attempts to fix the problem with the help of both the affected manager and employee. Both HR and management are considered "dispassionate players" in the negotiation because they're above the action and not considered to have any sort of personal agenda regarding the outcome. When progressive discipline or an employee transfer isn't feasible, then the mediator/broker may attempt to gently inject respect, dignity, and professionalism back into the working relationship by allowing the employee options and alternatives to remaining in an unhappy working relationship, often including an "easy out" exit strategy:

Olivia, you've worked as Ava's executive assistant for the past two years, and I don't believe that you or Ava has felt that this working relationship was a match made in heaven. In other words, sometimes it's just not the right personality mix or the right timing in people's lives, and the working relationship suffers. Would you agree that it hasn't been ideal for you? [*Yes.*]

Ava, you've shared your frustrations about Olivia's substandard job performance and inappropriate workplace conduct with me privately. I've recommended that you speak with Olivia directly, and you've done that on multiple occasions. So you're frustrated, too, right? [*Yes.*]

Okay, then it may be time to lay down our shields and extend the proverbial olive branch. There's enough work around here to sink a battleship. When you add the interpersonal friction that you've been both experiencing for the past year or so, it becomes unbearable. I don't want to minimize the importance of your working relationship together, but with all due respect, it's only work. I mean, when you think about families who lose their health or parents who have to see their children through serious illnesses—that's important in life. If we're not suffering from that kind of illness, we're lucky. So, let's keep that in perspective as we look at this workplace issue, okay?

Sometimes it's fair to say that it just isn't a good fit. What's important to me is that both parties feel like they're being supported and treated with dignity and respect right now. I don't want people feeling like their egos and self-esteem are being trashed. Life is simply too short for that.

Olivia, I need to share with you that Ava isn't going anywhere. She's a vice president, she's got long-term tenure with the organization, and senior management believes she's doing an excellent job. That's an important point for you, as her executive assistant, to keep in mind as you consider your options. As an objective third party, it appears to me that you're not happy here. You seem to be disappointed in the management team. You appear not to enjoy your work. And I'm sure you feel like you're not appreciated or part of the team, at least at certain times. Am I correct? [Yes.]

Okay, so tell me your thoughts: Would leaving now on your own accord allow you an honorable exit strategy? Would exploring other opportunities outside the company while you're still employed here make sense for you at this point in your career? We'd be willing to allow you to begin interviewing at other companies as long as you make sure that our work comes first and that we're given at least twenty-four hours' notice of an upcoming interview. I'm mentioning this only because I don't want you to feel like you need to feign illness or conjure up doctors' and dentists' appointments if you've got an interview coming up. I'd rather we all be above board and that you let us help you. More important, I want you to feel like you have options and choices in situations like this. You don't have to decide now, but please give some thought to how I may be able to help you with and through this.

One other thing, Olivia . . . I want you to know that this is strictly up to you. If you'd like our support to either resign on your own terms now or to begin looking for other work, then we'll help you. If not, that's okay too. We'll do everything we can to help you reinvent your working relationship with Ava and to feel more appreciated for your efforts. I just want you and Ava to feel better about working with each other if you choose to stay. I also want to give you these additional options, Olivia, because it's better that we discuss these things openly rather than leave them unsaid. Does that sound like a reasonable approach to the challenges we're facing? [*Yes.*]

This velvet glove approach typically lowers the tension in the relationship immediately. The logic to this intervention is simply this: it's always better to let people know where they stand. When people feel they are being treated professionally and respectfully, they'll typically respond in kind. Although delivering a message like this can be confrontational, it's therapeutic. After all, most people would prefer to be told that their manager would prefer that they take their marbles and play on somebody else's team. That's a much better alternative than having to "divine" from their manager's actions that they're not wanted anymore.

Are there downsides to this intervention technique? On one hand, yes: you never know exactly how people will respond because principle can easily get in the way. As such, they may be looking to find fault in order to cause greater drama (think lawsuits). On the other hand, as long as the third-party mediator is careful to ensure that the employee understands that this is *her* decision (thereby avoiding a constructive discharge claim later down the road), this intervention should work well. People need to hear how others feel about them. Most employees will appreciate the opportunity to hear about problems concerning them in an open and honest forum.

Still, there's one additional hurdle that you have to bear in mind: once you "show your hand" as an employer, the worker will quickly put two and two together if you ultimately terminate her for cause shortly afterward. This could end up triggering a wrongful termination and retaliation lawsuit. After all, the record could be interpreted as follows: "My department head and HR encouraged me to resign, and when I said no, they found a way to fire me." Okay, fair enough. But with HR and senior leadership working in tandem to offer the individual a respectful way out of the organization or at least the flexibility to interview elsewhere if she chooses, then most workers will respond in kind and avoid the retaliation argument. But proceed with caution and reach out to qualified legal counsel before initiating a meeting like this—for the sake of the record you're creating and especially if you suspect that the individual may be inclined to litigate.

The question, of course, is how often does this approach work? It depends. In this author's experience, it's an 80-20 game: 20 percent of the time employees choose to resign on the spot or agree to begin looking immediately for other work. That may not seem like a great track record, but if you look longer term, you'll find that many employees will simply leave the company quietly within three or four months after a meeting like this. After all, no matter how angry employees are at the company, they'll come to realize that fighting an uphill battle makes little sense. When angry people are treated respectfully, their anger dissipates. And when the anger and drama are removed from the equation, they often feel less inclined to stay with your company "on principle." More important, they'll typically leave peacefully on their own terms without all the histrionics and threats of lawsuits.

You can tell anybody anything—it's *how* you say it that matters. Both the involved supervisor and employee will appreciate your caring and objective approach to a difficult meeting like this. After all,

involved management is all about getting to the truly human concerns at hand—issues that may have been left unaddressed for far too
long. You'll simultaneously support your management team and allow your employees to take back control of their careers. That's what
enlightened leadership is all about.

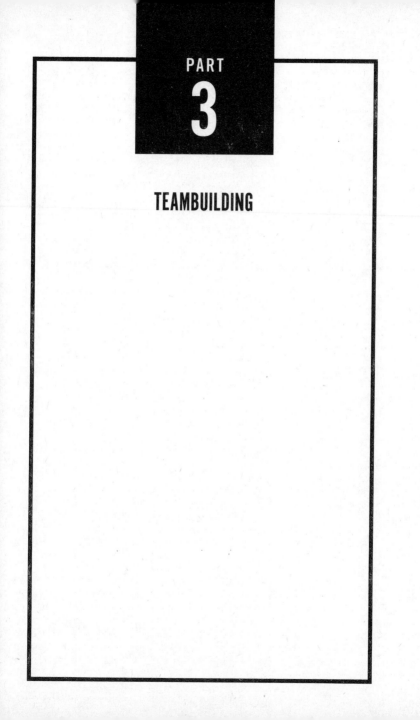

PART
3

TEAMBUILDING

THE IMPORTANCE OF TEAMWORK, CAMARADERIE, AND COOPERATION

Communication, teamwork, and cooperation are critical aspects of workplace performance because almost everyone has to work in groups of some sort. Even lab scientists who dedicate their research time to growing specimens in Petri dishes have to interact with colleagues, managers, and administrators within their hospital or research facility.

It's never enough to simply focus on your employees' *performance*; you need to ensure that your employees are equally responsible for their *conduct*—their ability to get along with others and make others feel welcome in their presence. In fact, their conduct is sometimes more important than their performance! That's because poor attitudes and aggressive and hostile behavior in the workplace negatively affect others and pull morale down—not to mention exposing companies to lawsuits for hostile work environment claims.

Here are the characteristics of people who show their willingness to cooperate, get along, and work together in teams:

■ They are open, honest, and straightforward (not secretive) and share information and knowledge willingly and readily with others; they build bridges based on trust and open communication.

▦ They welcome (and even solicit) constructive feedback. They listen actively and respond respectfully; they treat others with dignity and respect.

▦ They provide timely feedback and follow-up to others, both internally and externally.

▦ They remain open-minded and willing to entertain others' ideas; they treat no suggestion or request as trivial or minor; and they create a work environment based on inclusiveness, welcoming others' suggestions and points of view.

▦ They constantly look for common ground and encourage collaboration among team members; they resolve interpersonal conflicts without drama or angst; they build consensus with their coworkers and strive for the team to feel united in reaching a common goal; and they share the glory of success and attribute achievements to the team's effort (rather than any one person's).

▦ They capitalize on the specific talents of team members, and they provide encouragement (even if constructive criticism is necessary).

▦ They welcome positive confrontation rather than sweeping things under the rug; they confront problems head-on but in a firm and constructive manner; and they engage appropriately when in disagreement, and debate respectfully and in a spirit of good faith cooperation.

▦ They assume good intentions until proven otherwise and always look to bring out the best in others.

▦ They build consensus via shared decision-making.

▦ They foster a sense of shared accountability and group responsibility.

▦ They celebrate successes and recognize and appreciate others' contributions.

These are the attitudes, behaviors, and work habits you want to encourage in your employees.

If that's not clear enough, here are the behaviors you want to *avoid, prevent, and change* because you *don't* want people on your team who:

- Clearly prefer to work alone
- Avoid group-related assignments
- Hog information and resources
- Do not support or help others who are facing challenges
- Fail to interact with the team on a collegial basis
- Do not give credit where credit is due
- Cherry-pick the more appealing assignments
- Discourage their coworkers from volunteering ideas
- Shoot down untested suggestions and recommendations
- Demonstrate a domineering work style
- Resist new ideas or suggestions simply because "that's not the way we do that around here"
- Take credit for other team members' contributions
- Become antagonistic when their authority is challenged
- "Talk over" those with conflicting opinions

The examples above are provided for a reason: not only to describe and define those who exhibit teamwork, camaraderie, and cooperation but as a checklist and benchmark to determine which employees excel in these areas versus those who fail to engage with others appropriately. Simply put, all employees are responsible for creating and maintaining a friendly and inclusive work environment. Everyone on a team should exhibit these traits to an acceptable degree.

Too many times, top-producing sales representatives, as an example, believe that none of these behavioral expectations apply to them as long as their sales numbers continue to soar. Their assumptions could not be further from the truth. Yes, their performance is a significant indicator of their overall contribution to your organization. But what if their achievement comes at the expense of mistreating new sales reps who pose any sort of threat? Is that still acceptable? What if the branch rarely produces sales results above this individual contributor's deliverables because there is no room for anyone else's success? What if the branch suffers from 100 percent turnover every year because this individual intimidates or bullies others?

Unfortunately, the branch will rarely produce more than this top sales rep's contributions. And that's a major loss for your organization because while your office may have the capacity for eight sales reps, no one can survive working next to the "top performer" who heckles and cajoles his peers. There are many examples of this—not just in the sales realm—but the point remains the same: if individual contributors do not or cannot positively influence those around them and contribute to the broader team's morale, then you don't have a real sales "branch"—you simply have an individual sales rep who wastes the resources of the seven other desks around him.

Always consider both performance *and* conduct when looking at any employee's net contribution to your organization. Don't be misled by stellar sales performance or individual contributions; the team should be the core of your focus, not any particular contributor on it. When you have this "rebel sales syndrome" on your hand where the highest contributor is also your most problematic conduct problem, strategize with your boss and with human resources to turn that person around or move him out of the organization. True, your branch sales will take a temporary hit while you rebuild a new team, but it will likely be worth the time and investment to grow the branch's capacity. After all, you shouldn't be paying for office space that allows for eight sales desks when only one person performs consistently. It may be better to close the branch and allow that individual contributor to work from home since he can't get along with peers and associates and in fact weighs as a net negative, toxic influence on everyone else.

Leaders who excel at team turnarounds have to sometimes make difficult decisions like this. As always, line up your internal allies (senior management and human resources), use sales metrics and numbers to make your case in terms of lost sales potential from total turnover, and make the tough decision to move out those who refuse to engage in supporting their peers and the team as a whole. No employee has the discretion to waive their obligation of conduct and behavior because their performance is so high. To permit such toxicity to persist not only reflects poorly on your overall culture and corporate reputation but incentivizes others to model similar selfish and harmful behaviors as they come to assume that "this is the way things work in this organization."

16

HELPING YOUR TEAM LEARN, GROW, AND DEVELOP PROFESSIONALLY

Demographics is destiny. Demographers, social scientists, academics, and research think tanks that study Generation-Y "Millennials" and Generation-Z "Zoomers" have found certain core principles that drive these forty-and-under cohorts that now make up half of the US workforce. The top five values of these two generations consistently show up as:

- Diversity, equity, and inclusion
- Corporate social responsibility
- Work-life balance and flexibility
- Environmentalism
- Professional and career development

Organizations would be wise to listen to these priorities and build corporate programs around them to meet the needs and expectations of these quickly growing cohorts. What this looks like in your organization is a critical factor that can impact recruitment, retention, discretionary effort, and ultimately workforce ROI (return on investment).

Career and professional development sometimes gets neglected because of the demands and even crises that many organizations face. In light of layoffs and other challenges, companies' key goals remain staying in business and meeting payroll. That said, however, career and professional development remains a key imperative to these cohorts. If you want them to keep working effectively and together (and you do!), this is an important aspect of management that you should not overlook.

As a new manager, you'll need to hone your coaching skills and establish discussions with your employees about their achievements and areas for professional development, educational opportunities, and the like. The ideal approach might look like this:

Step 1: Annual performance review and the setting of performance goals for the upcoming year.

Step 2: Quarterly touch-base meetings (known as "individual development plans") to discuss accomplishments, progression toward goals, roadblocks, and pivots in planning.

Step 3: Annual self-evaluations about two weeks before performance-review meetings and a new round of goal-setting.

The questions that follow can be used at any of these three intervals and can be reintroduced during one-on-one conversations at any point. Begin your discussion with an employee with simple questions that invite conversation, such as:

▓ What are you working on and interested in learning more about at this point in your career development?

▓ On a scale of one to ten, ten being the best, how well are your career and professional interests connecting to the work you're doing day in and day out?

- On a scale of one to ten, how would you grade your overall contributions to the team and the organization in terms of being able to do your best work every day?
- What would you say are three adjectives that your most respected critic might use to define or describe you as a leader or as an individual contributor?

Listening to each employee during these conversations is key. Allow the employee to interpret the questions, work through them aloud, and reflect and respond. Giving a little less advice and asking a few more questions may be more challenging than you think. But if your goal truly is to serve as a mentor and coach to your team members, then listening more effectively should become your own key focus in personal and professional development.

For some, their focus may be on further education and finishing their degree. For others, promotions and earning more money may be key. But different motivators play a key role at different points in people's careers, so expect answers like these as well:

Work-life balance

The opportunity to work in a hybrid on-site/home setup

The potential to learn more about the broader organization, including transfers to international units

The acquisition of new technical skills, including new licenses and certifications

Whatever the case, you won't know until you ask. That's why one-on-one quarterly meetings are so important. The essence of coaching lies in unlocking others' potential. Inspire employees to adopt new habits. Encourage them to think of you not only as their boss but also as their career mentor and coach. Ask them how you can help them focus on building their strengths and codifying their achievements. The stronger their achievement mindset and the accomplishments they garner, the better for your department and company.

17

DELEGATION AS A MEANS OF TEAM DEVELOPMENT
GOOD FOR YOU, GOOD FOR YOUR TEAM

Managing in lean times requires special skills. Overly stressed managers sometimes feel that they're at the end of their rope because the workload appears all too often to be overwhelming. Sure, managers can handle increased hours, heightened workloads, and minimal (if any) compensation rewards for fairly sustained periods of time. But the reality is that the workplace has been exceptionally challenging since the new millennium began due to multiple financial crises and a global pandemic, and too many managers are simply running out of steam.

Using delegation as a skill to both lighten your workload and develop your team's leadership and performance muscle sounds like a great idea. But it has to be done right, and it might take more effort and attention than you might otherwise expect.

For example, we're not talking about delegating what you do not want to do: that would be perceived as selfish, and that's not the type of delegation that builds subordinates' strengths and provides greater opportunities for increased responsibilities. Instead, this is about delegating what you're good at in order to help others gain opportunities and build their own skills in kind. That approach to delegation is truly selfless, provides "stretch" opportunities for those being mentored, and encourages career growth and professional development. Be aware, though: it takes time to develop people, and you may very well end up spending more time with the delegation exercise than if you simply did the work yourself.

If you pride yourself on being a selfless leader, someone who puts others' needs ahead of your own and expects them to respond in kind, or someone who would encourage your employees to pursue other opportunities, either within or outside of your organization if it's a healthy move for them, then using delegation for career development makes sense. That's because delegation, in its highest sense, requires you to potentially give up something that you're comfortable with or enjoy doing.

For example, if you're a finance manager who enjoys budgeting for expatriate relocation assignments overseas or a legal department head who enjoys conducting your company's code of conduct training, then you might not want to assign those responsibilities to others. Likewise, if you see your highest value to your company in your relationships with the senior management team and pride yourself on the internal network you've developed over the years, then it might be somewhat threatening to integrate a subordinate into your network. That's why it's critical that you assess your own management style before undergoing an exercise like this. Be sure you're aware of what you'd be willing to delegate before making any commitments to your staff.

Wanting to delegate to people is both a natural inclination and a learned behavior, often depending on the corporate culture and degree of nurturing that you've personally experienced. On the other hand, you can't delegate until you understand who among your subordinates is ready to accept the opportunity to learn new skills. Assess your staff members by determining who may be ready for greater responsibility and meet with those individuals to learn what motivates them. Use the following checklist in a one-on-one meeting to ask each high-potential employee what motivates him or her most on a scale of one to six according to these general factors:

PERSONAL MOTIVATORS	
___ Career progression through the ranks/ promotion	___ Acquisition of portable management, administration, and leadership skills
___ Lateral assumption of increased job responsibilities/skill broadening	___ Work-life balance (that is, "living to work" versus "working to live")
___ Acquisition of new technical skills (typically requiring outside training or certification)	___ Money and other forms of compensation

Now, before you jump too quickly on the money option, remember that, within reason, people primarily work for the "psychic" income involved, not for the money. And as much as readers tend to minimize this reality, the truth is that most people who enjoy their work, like their boss and coworkers, and feel satisfied and engaged at work will not put money at the top of their list. Whether you choose to express it or not, you are basically asking your employee, "If you could focus on one area where you'd like to develop your own skills or gain more experience to broaden your resume and prepare for your next move in career progression (here or elsewhere), what would you want?" Understanding their key motivators and drivers will help you determine what you can delegate and how you can manage the process together.

Delegation may take the form of technical, managerial, or administrative skills. But it's not simply a matter of passing along responsibilities and then forgetting about it. The delegation itself becomes the focus of the exercise. It binds your subordinate to you throughout the period of implementation. So, set the following expectations at the point you delegate:

- ■ What exactly are your expectations in overseeing this project? What's your initial plan of attack in assuming responsibility for your new project? What parameters or boundaries would you place around this project if you were to accept it?

▪ How often do you plan on keeping me informed with status updates, and how would you prefer to communicate your progress?

▪ What are the measurable outcomes so that we know that you've achieved your goals?

Are there limitations or caveats to using delegation as a motivational staff development tool? Yes. First, you've got to know yourself. Be careful not to ask subordinates to volunteer information regarding their career goals if you're truly not prepared to give up some of your current responsibilities. You probably already have a general idea about what your people might request.

Second, be careful not to overload your staff. Sure, delegation potentially makes your job easier because you get to share your workload, but this exercise must be managed purposefully. If subordinates might perceive your efforts as self-serving or if they are afraid to say no to anything you assign them, then you may not be ready to use delegation as a career development tool. There must be a foundation of trust and mutual respect in your working relationship before this mentoring exercise gets initiated.

When staff members develop new skills and feel respected and recognized by their bosses, they stay put and find new ways of reinventing themselves in light of your organization's changing needs. In essence, your up-front investment in assessing your staff and taking the time to learn about their personal motivators will make your job easier and save you time over the long run, and there are few opportunities in life that allow you to work that smart. Such are the elements of enlightened leadership and proactive management.

18

REMOTE LEADERSHIP
MANAGING THE UNSEEN

With better and faster technology, remote employment remains on the rise, bringing with it greater flexibility in corporate hiring practices and workers' career management goals. It also requires a different set of leadership skills to motivate and engage employees who work with more independence than the US workforce has ever known before.

On the one hand, studies show that remote employees actually perform at a higher level because of greater flexibility and a healthier work-life balance. On the other hand, workers admit to feeling lonelier and socially isolated, and in many cases overlooked, as the out-of-sight, out-of-mind syndrome kicks in for those who are more ambitious at gaining face time with senior leaders and opportunities for growth.

Where does that leave you in terms of finding a healthy rhythm and balance relative to communication, teambuilding, and problem-solving? How do you manage the "unseen workforce"? Should it make you a bit nervous to remain accountable for the performance output of team members who you simply don't see enough to truly know how they're performing and what they're doing throughout the day?

Fear not: everything we've discussed in this book and the others in this series applies to managing remote employees effectively. Whether we're discussing selfless leadership, engaged listening, career and professional development discussions, or delegating projects according to people's strengths, the rules remain the same. With one exception: your one-on-one time with your subordinates requires a more focused and purposeful approach.

Without the benefit of working side by side, going to lunch, and getting to know your team members more personally at the office watercooler, your approach to remote leadership should focus on gaining those same advantages, only now on a one-on-one basis versus a group or team basis. Yet communication and accountability go hand in hand. Let's look at a few practical ways to establish an ongoing rhythm and cadence for feedback and communication to make this work for you.

WEEKLY ONE-ON-ONE MEETINGS

First, schedule a fixed one-on-one meeting with each of your direct reports every week. Assuming you have a reasonable number of direct reports (that is, anywhere from one to seven), then one meeting per day with a member of your team makes for a good rhythm and opportunity for feedback. The minimum length should be fifteen minutes and can go longer based on needs or preferences. Ask:

- How is your week going so far?
- Are you on target to meet your preplanned goals, or are you falling behind anywhere?

- Will you need additional resources, or have you encountered any roadblocks that I can help with?
- Can I help facilitate any meetings with particular members of our organization?
- As far as your go-forward weekly plan, how are things looking? Have you identified your short-term goals; are your projects aligned; or do you see any backups or delays coming?

WEEKLY TEAM MEETINGS

In these meetings, you might lead the conversation like this:

Let's all go around one by one and discuss what we're working on, what's ahead of schedule, and what might potentially fall behind.

How are we progressing toward our quarterly team and individual goals? Do any of you see potential roadblocks or delays coming your way that the rest of us should be aware of?

How are you going about establishing relationships and communication hubs with your peers in order to keep from feeling alienated or disconnected from the group?

Let's do a postmortem on the week as a team, looking at what we could be doing better or at least what we could have done differently to get stronger results.

Are there any other topics you'd feel comfortable sharing with the team—either in terms of project status, adjusting our goals, or looking into some new types of initiatives we haven't discussed before?

QUARTERLY ACHIEVEMENT MEETINGS

As we wrap up the end of the second quarter, it's time for us to evaluate and review our Q2 goals and achievements. Remember, this works just like with a publicly traded company's financial reporting requirements: quarterly reports feed into the annual report, and there shouldn't be any surprises along the way since we're on top of things.

Who wants to go first in terms of sharing their project status or goal updates?

What can we celebrate from our Quarterly Achievement Calendar? And what should that celebration look like this time around?

Do we need to pivot on any of our projects or goals as we move into Q3, or are we still aligned correctly to meet our year-end goals?

Are you aware of anyone who should be nominated for an employee-of-the-quarter award or some other type of recognition?

If you could change one thing about how effectively we're working as a team, what would it be? (Also, please suggest some solutions that we can consider.)

Are there any new initiatives for Q3 that we didn't contemplate earlier in the year? Should we amend our annual goals for any reason?

Do you see the need to introduce any particular types of software, systems, checklists, templates, personal metrics dashboards, or anything similar to help us capture our achievements more efficiently?

What's the right amount of structure, direction, and feedback that you all prefer from me going forward? Is our remote-working relationship continuing to work for you? Is there anything you'd like to see change?

Note: Quarterly one-on-one meetings might call for the following questions:

What can I do to help you codify your achievements this past quarter to help you build out your annual self-evaluation form, resume, or LinkedIn profile?

Is there anything you're looking into right now to advance your education or pursue some sort of licensure or certification program that can fall under our tuition-reimbursement benefit?

Are you looking to expand your professional network by joining any particular societies or industry groups?

Is there anything I can support you with that ties your personal career interests and professional development to opportunities here at work—for example, exposure to other areas of the business, opportunities to specialize in particular areas or become an internal subject matter expert, or interest in being considered eligible for the organization's high-potential program?

In general, aim for clarity, transparency, and overcommunication when supervising remote workers. Teamwork and operational coordination standards will likely need to be higher for remote workers than for those whom you see and oversee in person on a daily basis. Such flexible working arrangements can create a much bigger talent pool in which you can cast your recruiting net, providing you with significant advantages and opportunities in tight labor markets.

Remember, however: out of sight cannot mean out of mind. Your team members must continue to feel connected and to sense an intimate partnership with the organization as a whole. As these questions demonstrate, there can be unique and creative ways to lead a remote team that draw from the best advantages of remote assignments while downplaying the negative aspects of remote work.

19

MANAGING MULTIPLE GENERATIONS OF EMPLOYEES

RAISING AWARENESS OF OTHERS' PERSPECTIVES AND POINTS OF VIEW

More than one in three American workers today are Millennials (adults ages twenty-five to forty), and 2015 is the year they surpassed Generation X to become the largest share of the American workforce, according to a new Pew Research Center analysis of US Census Bureau data. Further, for the first time in history, we have five generations in the workplace.

In fairness, the workplace has never been a single-generation monopoly. Junior workers have always come in to gain experience and work toward advancement. Senior workers have always served as supervisors and mentors. And there has always been some form of tension between the two. And that's to be expected. But workplaces generally employed Americans from two or (at maximum) three generations, not five. As one might expect, this phenomenon affects the workforce in both subtle and overt ways.

Just a few decades ago, most workers retired at age sixty-five. But today, many are staying in the workforce well into their seventies. Young workers, meanwhile, continue to enter the job market at an unrelenting pace. This convergence of multiple generations reveals differences in value systems that can lead to workplace clashes as members of different generations disagree about how to behave and perform at work. As they disagree, they can become frustrated by the very act of communicating with one another, a dangerous factor that can damage their ability to work together productively. A brief look at the five generations is important to understand just how they make up this multigenerational workforce.

THE STABILIZING TRADITIONALISTS: THE VETERAN GENERATION

Demographers generally define this generation as born up to 1945. While they are currently in their mid-seventies or older, many members of the veteran generation remain in the workforce. Some enjoy highly paid leadership positions, while others are forced to continue working for low wages because they cannot afford to retire. The veteran generation believes in doing as you are told and respects a command-and-control structure that centralizes power at the leadership level. This generation views conformity as virtuous, an act of self-sacrifice, and communal responsibility.

THE TRANSFORMATIONAL BABY BOOMERS

This enormous generation—seventy-seven million in total—was born from 1946 to 1964. They were born to American soldiers who came home from World War II, purchased homes, and happily created families. Baby boomers had much greater access to higher education than their parents, they found more financial success as a result, and they believed in the American dream. They relish authority and seek out positions of power. They experienced a golden age of prosperity, although they have been challenged in their later years since pensions vanished and they failed to save adequately for retirement. As a result, baby boomers have largely stayed at work, and younger generations can feel frustrated, unable to advance because baby boomers are not retiring on schedule.

"ENTREPRENEURIAL" GENERATION X

Demographers identify this generation as being born from 1965 to 1979. They're a small generation of only forty-six million—the smallest of the five generations in the workplace, sometimes leading to problems with succession planning. Gen Xers graduated from college just in time to face the jobless recovery that followed the mid-1990s recession. Many watched their parents get laid off or struggle financially, and upon graduation, they experienced challenges obtaining meaningful employment and career paths themselves. As a result, Gen X's perspective on the business world is sometimes described as cynical and skeptical. As a generational force, then, Gen Xers prefer to work more independently, which can be interpreted as resistant to authority or even insubordinate. Like their Generation Y and Generation Z brethren, Gen Xers are described as having a slightly hedonist bent and don't necessarily live to work; they work to live and may not feel as inclined to sacrifice their own happiness for the good of the team.

GENERATION Y
("MILLENNIALS" OR "THE NET GENERATION")

Born roughly between 1980 and 1995, Gen Yers' sense of empowerment (sometimes interpreted by the other generations as entitlement) spurs them to seek experiences that transcend the ideals of a traditional career path. They search for employment with the goal of finding experiences that satisfy them, and they can be peaceful about letting jobs go—whether they're laid off or leave on their own. Gen Y perceives lack of job security as normal, so they've chosen to be satisfied by opportunities that come their way for as long as they last. Gen Y's tech-infused upbringing created a generation that excels at multitasking. They're accustomed to juggling phone calls, emails, texts, and social media posts. They believe that business should focus on a societal purpose and the environment, not just be in business to make a profit. They strive to support causes that align with their values and personal belief system. In fact, they have forced companies to rethink flexibility, meetings, and the use of cubicles.

GENERATION Z (SOMETIMES REFERRED TO AS "ZOOMERS")

The Gen Zers were born between 1996 and 2012. As of the time of this writing, the oldest are in their mid-twenties. The first truly global generation, thanks to social media, this cohort grew up in a post-9/11 world, witnessed the first Black American elected president, became acutely aware of school shootings and the coronavirus pandemic, and was inundated with the concept of "fake news" on the internet. It's likely a bit too early to document their core values because this young generation is still defining itself. Many describe themselves as the hardest-working generation and are inclined to entrepreneurial endeavors. They live online, believe in corporate social responsibility and the environment, and have no knowledge of the world as it existed before smartphones.

SOLUTIONS TO MULTIGENERATIONAL WORKFORCE CHALLENGES

With such an eclectic mix of generations, worldviews, and experiences, how can any manager hope to create harmony and alignment in the workplace? Success in this realm, as in so many others, stems from open and honest communication, respect, and recognition. While differences will clearly exist in terms of views on authority, leadership and communication styles, and feelings about work-life balance, the following factors may foster a positive atmosphere in your workplace:

- ■ *Cross-generational mentoring and coaching:* This helps acclimate older workers to new technologies and helps younger workers gain wisdom as they benefit from older workers' experiences. (Watch the movie *The Intern* with Robert DeNiro and Anne Hathaway: you'll love the message and see how multiple generations learned to work together as a team.)

- ■ *Collaborative and rotational work assignments and projects:* These bring people together quite naturally and align them in a common cause. Remain cognizant of building teams with this type of diversity in mind. Diverse ideas and opinions tend to strengthen a team's final recommendations because of the inclusive nature of so many disparate points of view.

- ■ *Flexible work schedules:* These offer new alternatives to getting work done thanks to technology. The COVID-19 pandemic in 2020 and 2021 made remote work a staple of business life worldwide. Encourage flexible teams and multiple outlets for communication and remote teambuilding to capitalize on this new trend, which appears to create greater performance and productivity than traditional nine-to-five work settings.

- ■ *Opportunities to cross-train on the latest technologies:* In-house technical training is helpful to any team, but it's an excellent stretch assignment for high-potential employees who enjoy teaching and public speaking.

- ■ *Training workshops on leadership and communication:* Any of the content from this book or any others in the *Paul Falcone*

Workplace Leadership Series can be used to develop content on leadership and communication. Get people talking about communication in terms of what works and what can be changed. Encourage open discussions about how to ratchet communication up a notch in your shop.

▪ *A social atmosphere of community at work, including environmental awareness and social causes that make the world a better place:* Millennials and Gen Z make up almost half of the US workforce as of this writing. In the next decade, that figure will shoot up closer to 60 percent. It's in every organization's best interests to get to know this powerful combination and what its top priorities are: diversity and inclusion, good corporate citizenship, the environment, career and professional development, and work-life balance and flexibility. Make these staples of your organizational voice and pronounce them loudly during the recruitment process.

▪ *Teambuilding events that heighten awareness of others' backgrounds:* There are myriad books written on teambuilding exercises, and for good reason: this remains a critical imperative in the workplace. Bond your teams by addressing differences and developing areas of agreement and commonality. Add a "What Can We Learn from One Another?" exercise to keep the door open to new possibilities for increased interaction and learning.

▪ *Networks of cross-functional councils and boards that serve as a primary source of leadership and decision-making:* Committee work naturally brings people together from across organizations. It represents an excellent opportunity for high-profile exposure as well as an opportunity to truly make a difference in your organization's future. Committees also give senior leaders an opportunity to pass along wisdom to younger generations, ensuring a healthy transition of power in succession planning.

■ *Social-networking tools that build relationships, increase*
collaboration, and enhance employee engagement: New tools are
rampant in the workplace—communication tools, performance
feedback apps, employee recognition software, and even artificial
intelligence and smart apps that mimic human behavior and
project future outcomes. Get on board by sharing, teaching, and
having fun with new tools and apps, but remember that nothing
replaces good old-fashioned human judgment and the warmth
of human touch.

If a single project team spans several generations, communication
could become a major stumbling block. Encourage team members to
let one another know how they prefer to communicate. By sharing
how—and how often—they plan to be in touch with one another,
teams can anticipate and avoid communication gaps before they occur.

Despite their vast differences, it's important to remember that generations can work together effectively. Each brings a unique viewpoint
and skill set to the table. And if they can be persuaded to communicate
openly with one another and respect their differences, there is no workplace challenge that a diverse but united team cannot master.

To foster a more collaborative environment, embrace employees'
differences, not from a sense of toleration but as a source of strength.
Leverage the energy and creative enthusiasm that the newest generations bring to the workplace. Rely on the wisdom of elder generations
who overcame challenges unknown to the younger cohorts. Think
carefully about succession planning, and coach up-and-coming managers and executives to work effectively with all the generations they
lead. Know that many of the ideas outlined above work just as well in
a remote environment as they do in person. Thanks to technology,
the ability to communicate and bond from a distance has never been
greater.

20

THE IMPORTANCE OF FOSTERING A DIVERSE AND INCLUSIVE WORKFORCE

New managers face many questions and outdated assumptions surrounding diversity, equity, and inclusion (DEI)—for example:

- Will we ever achieve true diversity, equity, and inclusion?
- Is it realistic or artificial in terms of forcing placements and promotions of diverse candidates within your organization, including your board of directors?
- Is DEI just race-based affirmative action from the 1960s in another form?

Here's the reality: as outlined in chapter 19, Millennials and Gen Z make up a significant percentage of the US workforce. Wise employers will be served well to address their needs. And a workforce that is diverse in terms of people, ideas, and cultures registers right at the top of the list in terms of what attracts and motivates the Gen Y and Gen Z cohorts.

Focusing your organization on this key goal and advertising your commitment to it will likely help you attract and retain talent successfully. It's that simple.

Further, McKinsey & Company and other consulting firms, as well as myriad business schools, have confirmed that organizations with diverse boards, leadership teams, and workforces continue to outperform companies with more homogeneous employee and board constituents. Why? Because organizations whose decision- and strategy-making employees look like their clients, customers, and consumers will likely be more in tune and aligned with their needs and wants.

What's the reality look like for young workers observing work-force patterns and the current "state of the state" in corporate America these days? They see, according to HarperCollins Leadership Essentials:

- Only 3.3 percent of managers in US companies are Black men.
- In twenty years, the number of women in leadership positions hasn't changed.
- Seventy-eight percent of employees believe their workplaces lack diversity at leadership levels.

Further, according to the Society for Human Resource Management, Black individuals make up 13 percent of the US population but account for only 8 percent of employees in professional roles. They hold only 3.2 percent of all executive or senior leadership roles and less than 1 percent of all Fortune 500 CEO positions. In short, corporate America's efforts to increase diversity appear to be lacking significant results.

Of course, DEI extends far beyond race and gender to include, among other things, age, disability, sexual orientation, veteran status, and much more. It's understandable that you can't simply snap your fingers and change company demographics overnight. But you can demonstrate your efforts in better incorporating a diversity of ideas, opinions, and thoughts by engaging in and highlighting your organization's efforts surrounding:

- Unconscious bias (also known as *implicit bias*) training: a popular approach to diversity awareness training
- Data usage, particularly in terms of internal promotion and transfer rates as well as high-potential employee and succession planning exercises
- Allyship, especially in the form of Employee Resource Groups, in which employees who share a common characteristic (such as gender, ethnicity, religious affiliation, lifestyle, or personal interests) come together voluntarily to foster a more diverse and inclusive workplace aligned with their values—for example, by focusing on corporate social responsibility, environmental sustainability, and military-to-veteran transition, to name a few
- Mentorship and sponsorship, including high-potential programs, community ambassadors, and new-hire "buddies"— all excellent opportunities to mentor and be mentored
- Retention efforts, via turnover-risk analysis for certain employee cohorts, often gleaned from employee opinion surveys, climate surveys, or peer groups
- Community engagement, typically via volunteer days
- Corporate social responsibility, often connected with community engagement, including adopting nonprofit causes for sponsorship and fundraising

In some states, larger-scale initiatives are underway to raise awareness of our differences and encourage a more inclusive and tolerant society. In California, for example, all public boards of directors must have had at least one female member as of 2019. As of 2021, female director representation increased, depending on the size of the board—the larger the board, the larger the number of female representatives.

The point of all this? First, public pressure from investors and shareholders is forcing publicly traded corporations to rethink their approach to diversity representation and equality of opportunity. Second, and even more critical, is that your clients, customers, and consumers demand that you speak their language. The greater the diversity of your business team, the stronger the chances that you will meet and exceed customers' expectations.

Find the approaches that will make the most sense for you and your organization to adopt and then publicize your efforts loudly and proudly—to your own employees, to job applicants, and to your customer base. DEI is no longer a nice-to-have: it is now a critical business imperative that organizations may suffer under if they fail to realize and capitalize on its value.

For additional ideas and considerations regarding building your organization's DEI practices, see book 1 of this series on *Workplace Ethics*, topic 22.

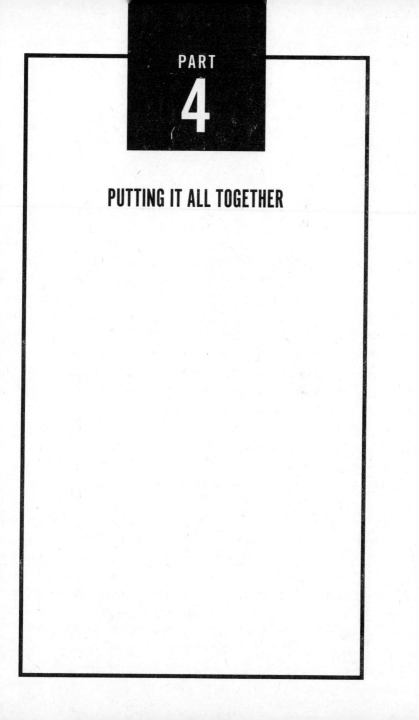

PART

4

PUTTING IT ALL TOGETHER

21

ESTABLISHING KEY METRICS
TO DRIVE YOUR BUSINESS

Numbers tell fascinating stories and shouldn't be overlooked in your own leadership development or that of your employees. Even more important, they appeal to the C-level—the senior executive leadership team at your company that is responsible for business growth and solutions to the constantly changing needs of the organization. Some companies' operations lend themselves to analytical operational overviews and the key drivers that make the business work, but it's surprising that more leaders don't take the time to assess key business metrics and build their own individual development plans around them. After all, increasing revenue, decreasing expenses, saving time, and developing new systems and practices are what every function in corporate America is ultimately responsible for. Your challenge lies in identifying the metrics that drive your department or unit and then quantifying your results in terms of numbers and percentages.

Only your executive leadership team can tell what critical success factors, key performance indicators, and key behavioral indicators drive your organization or your particular department or division. But it may be well worth asking for. Planning for performance management requires strategic thinking and analytical measurement and lines up as follows:

■ **Critical Success Factors** (CSFs) are driven by business imperatives and may be any of four types:

Industry-specific factors speak to your trade, industry, or line of business and are likely fairly unique.

Environmental considerations may be based on (a) business climate, (b) the economy, or (c) technological advances.

Strategic considerations encompass changes in technology, demographic trends, and even international trade agreements that have the potential to significantly affect your distribution model and market access.

Organizational factors can include an aging workforce or union influence, for example, that poses a potential human capital threat in the near term or in the next three to five years.

■ **Key Performance Indicators** (KPIs) build on CSFs and affect every organization's mission and objectives. Set the KPI to meet your CSF with the following considerations in mind:

KPIs must be aligned with corporate organizational goals and be quantifiable (clear/focused).

What you can measure you can achieve, or what gets measured gets managed.

KPIs must be straightforward and unambiguous and focused on strategic outcomes.

> Measurement toward a goal for monitoring a process is
> equally important; for example, by measuring an input (raw
> materials) or an output (sales).

Let's look at an example where curiosity clearly inspired a divisional HR leader looking to solve a long-term problem at the blood bank where she worked: driving more donor participation at her division's donor centers. By mapping out problems on a whiteboard and looking at the challenges currently facing the procurement division, the HR team was able to take an objective look at low donor turnout challenges and then develop a smart scorecard system that turned out to be fun and creative. Sharing ideas with senior leaders who might want to partner with you is where inspiration meets creativity and innovation, and the end results can be remarkable. Here's the scenario:

This company that collects human blood plasma has donor centers located throughout the nation. Donor centers vary fairly widely in size from twenty beds on the smaller end to upward of a hundred beds in larger facilities. A small team of general managers (GMs) oversees a larger team of regional managers (RMs) who in turn are responsible for approximately six donor centers each.

The challenge stemmed from the donor centers producing sporadic results. Some of the larger ones had lackluster donation volumes, while some of the smaller centers were on fire, constantly breaking records. How were the GMs to raise productivity of the lackluster centers and maintain the productivity of the super producers? Further, how could the GMs focus the efforts of their RMs on shepherding each of their donor centers to higher levels of performance and unit output?

As in many cases in multiple industries, the problem wasn't with technology, budgets, or even competition. The challenge came from—you guessed it—the lack of an aligned people strategy. In other words, human capital—the people factor in any organization—is often the ultimate lever in productivity and profitability. It turns out that the key determinant of any center's performance was linked directly to the regional manager's knowledge of the center and familiarity with its people.

HR was able to develop a scorecard that measured many of the key people drivers of each center, and that made it easy for the RMs to compare one center to another within their geographic region. A simplified version of a scorecard looked like this:

DONOR CENTER 1		
DEMOGRAPHICS	**TURNOVER**	**RECRUITMENT**
Average age Average tenure Average salary Average weekly overtime	Annual voluntary turnover Annual involuntary turnover Annual total turnover Exit Interview Score: (1) company, (2) supervisor, (3) team	Average time-to-fill Cost-per-hire Source cost analysis #/% Internal promotion
CROSS-TRAINING #/% Phlebotomists #/% Donor Processors #/% Plasma Processors	**HIGH-POTENTIAL EMPLOYEE(S)** #/% Ready to promote now #/% Ready to promote within 1 year #/% Ready to promote within 1–3 years	**AVERAGE MONTHLY DONATION VOLUME**

Notice that the only metric that was operational in nature and not people-related was the Average Monthly Donation Volume at the end of the scorecard. That served as the (performance) denominator in all calculations and comparisons that followed. Everything else relied in some form on leadership and people management.

The aha moment arrived when the corporate VPs, divisional GMs, and RMs could see how dashboards compared so easily across donor centers. All regional managers were able to hold one-on-one discussions with their donor center managers to track results from this simple leadership scorecard. Regional managers could easily compare all six donor centers within their scope of responsibility. General managers could compare eighteen to twenty-four donor centers within their purview. And divisional VPs could immediately gain access to the fifty to sixty donor centers within their scope of control. The comparisons were all neatly laid out on a simple Excel spreadsheet with multiple tabs. Here's what some of the conversations with donor center managers sounded like after regional managers tallied results across donor centers:

> Megan, the average tenure in your donor center is only nine months, and that's a concern to me. The average tenure in our region is 2.4 years and nationwide is 2.1 years. Likewise, your annual turnover is exceptionally high at 58 percent, relative to our region's 28 percent and our national turnover at 31 percent. Let's discuss turnover and see how we can build a plan together to review exit interviews and take a deeper look at why people may be leaving the center.

> Julio, I see it's taking ninety days to fill an open position in your donor center on average, which is more than double the regional average of forty-two days. How do you think keeping those positions open so long may be affecting morale on the rest of the team? Your overtime is also well beyond what we'd expect, so let's build a recruitment plan to backfill your job openings more aggressively and see if we can tighten up your overtime payouts at the same time.

> Sean, you haven't identified one high-potential employee in your donor center. That concerns me because I'm afraid you may not be focusing enough on career development and encouraging your staff members to enroll in the courses necessary to get double- or triple-certified. How can we remedy that?

> Rebecca, you've got the longest tenure of any donor center in our region. You have exceptionally low turnover, yet your plasma volume remains the lowest in the region. Do you think your team may be too complacent, and if so, how can we relight a fire underneath them to motivate them to perform at a higher level?

The truth is that problems driving production were stemming almost exclusively from human capital (people) challenges. Only by mapping key people issues on a whiteboard—tenure, internal promotion rate, cross-train rate, and the like—did the issues become clearer. Low volume plus high turnover was a deadly combination for one donor center; low volume plus high longevity was a problem for another, albeit for a different reason (complacent workers). What's more, superstar donor center leaders began to stand out: those with the highest percentage of volume-per-employee were asked to present on what makes their donor center particularly successful. Regional managers invited donor center leaders from other regions to address their teams. And most important, regional managers were more easily identified for GM roles.

Alignment, communication, succession planning, and leader acknowledgment and recognition soared. People felt better about their work. Regional managers visiting donor centers had a scorecard to review as soon as they arrived, congratulating those who reached significant anniversaries, were cross-trained in multiple areas, and were now identified as high-potential employees. And all it took was a bit of curiosity from an objective, fresh set of eyes to take a renewed look at the problem plaguing the organization to that point in time. HR business partners were likewise held accountable for measuring and managing their donor centers' human capital performance in terms of reducing turnover, incentivizing cross-training, and identifying high-potential employees. Alignment across all levels—GM, RM, donor center manager, and HR business partner—kept everyone on the same page with their eye on the ball. The divisional CEO couldn't have been happier, and the HR team truly demonstrated the value of leadership, communication, and teambuilding with the help of a simple Excel spreadsheet and a healthy dose of good old-fashioned curiosity.

22

HOW HR AND FRONTLINE MANAGERS CAN WORK TOGETHER TO REDUCE EMPLOYEE TURNOVER

Many organizations suffer from exceedingly high employee turnover—which often means there is a crisis of effective leadership and strong management. Too many employee opinion surveys cite leadership apathy, unfairness, and lack of recognition and communication as key culprits driving premature turnover. Obviously, those problems contribute to the challenges of building effective teams: if your employees are running out the door, you're not going to be able to get them to work together to achieve departmental or company-wide goals.

Needless to say, when that happens, the CEO and senior executive team will want HR to stop the hemorrhaging of employees. Before the HR manager does anything, though, HR should spend time with senior managers and staff members throughout the organization to learn firsthand about their assessments of the problem and their proposed solutions.

For example, there was a nagging situation facing a cable TV company with multiple regional call centers, each of which seemed to have its own reasons for high turnover: hot employment markets, racial tensions, and even religious conflicts that took place in a

Christian evangelical town that housed a large number of believers in witchcraft. Further, because of high turnover, employees appeared to be burned out and frustrated: in certain centers, they even took bets on how long a new hire would last before throwing in the towel.

Before doing anything else, the HR manager held meetings with key stakeholders in this order:

1. Senior vice president
2. General managers (that is, vice presidents)
3. Regional managers
4. Call center managers
5. Select employee focus groups

The feedback the HR manager received was fairly consistent: the key challenges were not external, as originally believed. The pressure of constantly being "overmonitored" by a computer system that measured the number of calls, the length of each call, the percentage of first-call resolutions, the ratio of escalated calls to higher tiers, and the like led to employee resentment and a constant feeling of being micromanaged. Employees stated they felt like they couldn't breathe, and managers agreed that the level of control made it feel like they were managing machines and cogs in a wheel rather than people.

From those meetings with the various leaders and focus groups, the HR manager also identified what might have triggered such high levels of employee dissatisfaction: leaders weren't hiring the right people, providing internal opportunities for growth, demonstrating any forms of recognition or appreciation, setting expectations appropriately, or holding workers accountable.

To remedy this situation, the HR manager proposed several programs that call center managers could lead (with the HR team's support):

- First, managers would rewrite their job postings to "sell" the company and attract better applicants. Applicant screening would be tightened, and in certain areas, employees were permitted to hold group interviews with finalist candidates.
- Second, managers would create a recruitment brochure featuring the company's history, career progression program, benefits, and specifics of the hiring process. A full campaign was launched surrounding the cross-training capabilities available, and a learning management system was rolled out, replete with self-paced videos to develop technical and leadership skills in addition to career progression materials.
- Third, managers created a one-page informational document on "What to Expect in Your First Ninety Days" that hiring managers would be able to share with candidates during interviews. The document explained the challenges of the role (in this case, dealing with cranky customers, sitting all day, and explaining how the computer monitoring system worked so there were no surprises later down the road). Also, a call center tour became the new standard, so applicants could observe the tier one resolution process, sit in on calls, and see firsthand the many internal departments (and opportunities) that existed.
- Finally, discussions surrounding how to work better with the computer automation system were scheduled. Employees were invited to share their ideas of how to work within the system without feeling like a number. They likewise suggested that the system be "gamified" to trigger recognition and appreciation of achievements when certain milestones were met (as opposed to simply pointing out problems).
- An ambassador (aka buddy) program was launched where high-potential employees were paired with new hires to guide them through their first ninety days, which ensured a smoother

transition into the company and a healthy sense of competition among ambassadors looking to ensure their mentees' success. The ambassador program later became the first step in the high-potential program that was eventually rolled out.

In addition, a look at the unique, key variables that made each location operate smoothly and efficiently was launched: implicit bias and respect in the workplace training programs were introduced, cross-training opportunities formalized, certification programs launched, and a step progression plan (up the ladder, as an employee gains more experience in a particular role) was designed to make each location more flexible and in tune with employees' needs. Finally, group and team exercises were planned to strengthen peer relationships and communication. The beauty in this solution was that it was at each center's fingertips the whole time: it simply took an outside impartial observer with a healthy dose of curiosity and goodwill to bring out these solutions and help codify them going forward. That's teamwork at its best.

Even if you're not in human resources with access to the entire organization's people results, there is typically so much you can do to reinvent the way your department or team operates. Start with team meetings and white butcher-block paper. Map out processing steps, highlight areas where backups typically occur, and ask your team for feedback and suggestions to streamline operations. If you don't ask, you simply won't know. And that's the beauty of effective leadership: you don't have to know! You simply need to create the space for people to provide input and suggestions. No one knows the workload, the shortcuts, and the land mines better than those in the trenches. When you're given the opportunity to lead them, acknowledge them. Recognize them. Ask for their input, especially in terms of what's working and what isn't. You won't have answers to all the problems right away, but you'll be able to build your own goals and quarterly achievement plan for your boss based on your team's findings and recommendations.

DEALING WITH EMPLOYEES IN CRISIS
A BLUEPRINT FOR POSITIVE MANAGEMENT INTERVENTION

Preventing violence and enhancing workplace safety are important to all employers. But instructing frontline leaders on how to deal with an employee crisis on a proactive basis sometimes gets short shrift. What do you do when you notice employees isolating themselves from the rest of the group? How do you deal with an employee who states that he's feeling suicidal? And what if your "suicidal" employee seems to go a step further and becomes potentially "homicidal"? These extreme situations don't occur often in the workplace. Still, most HR practitioners have dealt with many employees in crisis at some point in their careers, and now is the time to pass along that wisdom and build a methodology for addressing such a critical problem.

INVITING THE ISOLATED EMPLOYEE BACK INTO THE FOLD

Workers vulnerable to irrational acts typically appear as loners who are isolated from the rest of the group. These people often develop a "time clock" mentality in which they go through the motions of doing their jobs but are otherwise disengaged. Extending a helping hand to them can sometimes be a daunting task, so managers often avoid dealing with the issue.

Left in a vacuum void of information and two-way communication, however, these employees sometimes create their own versions of reality. Generally speaking, such individuals may tend to demonstrate a low level of self-awareness and an entitlement mentality that makes it difficult to approach them or gain their buy-in. As such, they may attribute negative intentions to others' actions where none were intended in order to justify their anger. What these loners may need is an opportunity to reconnect to the group and enjoy the social elements of work—recognition and appreciation for a job well done as well as a sense that they belong and can make a positive difference in the workplace.

Making it safe for solo players like this to reengage with their coworkers is no easy task. It begins by strengthening your own personal relationship with the individual as the group leader. It's then followed by encouraging group activities where participation is required, and you take the "outsider" under your wing and make it safer for everyone to interact more collaboratively. While there's no right or wrong way to do this, understand that players on all sides will naturally feel vulnerable if they need to engage more proactively with one another. Your job is to make it safe for them to feel vulnerable. And the best way to do that is to make yourself vulnerable and show everyone else that it's okay to feel that way. Your act of caring is enough, and it will speak volumes as to your character and compassion.

A key step is to meet with your staff members one on one to learn how they view the situation. Ask questions like these:

How would you grade our group in terms of camaraderie and teamwork? How do staff members get along with each other, and have you had any particular problems with other members of the group?

Are you aware of any particular historical problems among the team members, and could you tell me how they were or weren't resolved? Did anyone "disengage" after any particular incidents or otherwise appear to be isolated or abandoned from the group?

What would you recommend we do to better the situation?

I have to ask a favor of you. If I attempt to bring peace to both sides of this rift, would you support me and welcome the problem employee back into the fold?

More likely than not, you'll hear fairly consistent stories and explanations of the ongoing strife with each employee group, and you'll probably see both sides of the story objectively and have a better understanding of how the fallout came to be. With each individual's commitment to do her part in bettering the situation, it will then be time to hold a group meeting.

The group meeting might open like this:

Folks, we spend more time with our coworkers than we do with our families and friends, and there's certainly more than enough work to go around. What can make this unbearable for us, however, is allowing a negative environment to fester. If there's a lack of communication, harbored unresolved resentments, or a lack of respect for one another, then not only is work not going to be any fun—it's also not going to be particularly productive.

I've met individually with each of you to learn about issues historically affecting the group, and I want you to know that I'm holding each of you accountable for creating a work environment where everyone is treated with respect and dignity. I'm also holding you responsible for your own "perception management," meaning that it's not about being right or wrong. It's about ensuring that others understand your good intentions and are made to feel welcome and included in our department.

I realize that this situation may have taken years to get to this point, and it may take just as long to get to a point where there's mutual trust and respect in your interactions. But people tend to respond in kind, and if you treat others respectfully, they'll do the same for you. I'm here to ensure that that's the case, and I'll be here for each of you should you need me.

But I won't stand for any attempts to place blame on others. I also won't have any members of our staff feeling singled out or otherwise isolated from the rest of the team. Likewise, no tattletales, snitches, or gossipmongers allowed. If the problems continue, there will be disciplinary consequences. But if you support me in making this a more inclusive working environment, then we can discover new ways of adding value to our work. Can I count on your support?

Allowing people to feel safe will do more than anything to avert a potential crisis in the workplace.

EMPLOYEE ASSISTANCE PROGRAMS

What happens if, despite your best intentions, the isolated individual tells you he or she is feeling suicidal? If your company has an employee assistance program (EAP), you can say to the employee:

Chris, I want you to wait here with me while I call the EAP, because I'm not your best resource if you're feeling that way, and I know that Marilyn Jones at the EAP would certainly help. Okay?

Making a "formal" referral to the EAP (as opposed to a "voluntary" referral in which the employee self-refers) should almost always be done with the employee's consent.

But in extreme cases where a formal referral may be warranted, you must ensure that the employee has a job performance problem in addition to appearing to be mentally depressed, suicidal, or potentially hostile. In the case of formal referrals, you would discuss your perceptions of the work performance problems with the intake counselor on the front end (although not necessarily in front of the employee). With a signed release from the employee, the EAP will later be able to provide you with limited feedback about the individual's attendance, compliance, and prognosis.

In certain cases (for example, with potential workplace violence issues), you have the option of not permitting the individual back to work without a fitness-for-duty release from a licensed health-care practitioner. Such leaves are usually paid through the initial period of evaluation. Beyond that, employees typically use accrued time off to be compensated while receiving further treatment.

AMERICANS WITH DISABILITIES ACT LIMITATIONS AND CAVEATS

One caveat about "formal" EAP referrals: although they may certainly be justified in cases of threats of employee suicide, recent case law shows that formal EAP referrals have created burdens on employers under the Americans with Disabilities Act (ADA). Specifically, plaintiffs' attorneys have argued that, on the basis of a mandatory EAP referral, the employer did indeed *regard* the client as disabled. (The ADA and some state disability discrimination laws protect individuals who either have or are perceived as having a disability, including a mental disability.) Such an interpretation could become legally problematic should you then decide to take some adverse action (especially termination) against the employee.

In addition, you shouldn't mandate that an employee attend treatment sessions by threatening termination for not doing so. Such a requirement could appear to make an EAP referral an extension of your disciplinary authority and give rise to claims of disability discrimination based on a perceived mental disability, invasion of privacy, or misuse of confidential medical information in certain states. In short, when facing a challenge of this magnitude, retain the services of qualified employment defense counsel in advance (if possible). An ounce of prevention is worth a pound of cure, especially considering that the ADA allows for punitive damages in cases where disability discrimination may be involved.

PUT SAFETY FIRST

An extreme worker reaction might also result in veiled threats of homicide rather than suicide. For example, what if an employee came to your office one morning, placed a live shell of ammunition on your desk, and stated that her coworkers better not bother her today "if they know what's good for them"? Veiled threats like these are not uncommon in extreme cases.

Your first reaction would probably be to fire this person and ensure that he or she has no further access to company property. And that may be the best decision for your organization in the end. Still, it's probably best to make a record that you didn't overreact or jump to unfair conclusions. In such cases, placing the employee on a paid administrative leave might make the most sense. Explain your rationale to the employee this way:

Chris, I know you met with our EAP provider, and they gave us a written release for you to return to work. You also told me that you were feeling much better about work and about your relationship with your coworkers at that time. But the feelings that you're sharing with me right now raise some concerns, as I'm sure you understand, and I think it's best to send you home with pay while I discuss with my superiors how to best handle this. We'll call it an administrative leave and continue to pay you as though you were working full-time. I'll call you tonight at home.

I've got to ask a favor, though. The way that our company normally handles these things is to ask the employee to go straight home. I can't have you here at work while I do my objective fact-finding. Having you wait at home is always part of an administrative leave. Is that reasonable to you, and will you support that request?

[*Yes.*]

Gently escort the employee off the premises and alert security or take other reasonable steps to ensure your other workers' safety. Most employment lawyers will recommend that you tell the others that a threat, whether overt or veiled, was indeed made against them individually or as a group. You should likewise share the steps the company is taking to address the situation. But to protect the individual's privacy and to avoid later claims of defamation, you should limit disclosure of specifics only to those individuals with a need to know.

Bring these newfound threats to the attention of the EAP provider, and be sure to seek the advice of qualified legal counsel before moving to terminate. If you then choose to dismiss, do so over the phone within twenty-four to forty-eight hours. Send the employee's personal belongings and final paycheck to his or her home via courier. Include a letter that states that this person may no longer enter company property for any reason without the advance approval of the vice president of human resources or similar designee. The company attorney should approve the final draft of the letter. Finally, remember that EAPs are also an excellent resource for your other employees should they need someone to talk to. Most EAPs will agree to come on-site for group needs or at least conduct a group remote call or videoconference.

Leadership, teambuilding, and trust require full transparency. Employees need to know that you're being open and honest with them and are there to help them through challenges like this. Terminated employees must likewise be treated respectively and professionally so that they can move on in their careers, understanding that the company's decision wasn't personal and was simply driven by the timing and the fact pattern that was created. Speak your truth but soothe your words with peace. Share your message with compassion. Express what needs to be said with softness, with an open heart, and with an offer to help any time in the future. Remember, the truth can hurt, but it typically hurts a lot less if you care how it feels while saying it. That's what great leadership and communication are all about.

24

WHAT GOT YOU HERE WON'T GET YOU THERE

ASSESS YOURSELF TO BECOME A BETTER MANAGER

Bestselling author and leadership guru Marshall Goldsmith's book *What Got You Here Won't Get You There* addresses how personal habits and behaviors might stand in the way of reaching your next level of achievement. It likewise focuses on the transition from individual contributor to manager and the different skill sets that may be required. The book wisely proffers that the very characteristics that you believe got you where you are today—for example, the drive to win at all costs—may be what's holding you back from achieving your next step in career progression. The author proposes that professionals develop a "to-stop" list rather than a "to-do" list to climb beyond their own self-imposed limitations objectively and rationally.

Yes, we all may have our own unconscious habits that may stand in our way. How can we take a fresh look at ourselves, embracing the idea that change is easier than we might imagine—as long as we can demonstrate a little humbleness and openness on our parts to evaluate ourselves fairly and objectively? The answer, of course, is as broad and limitless as our openness to self-critical insight will allow. It can be found in a combination of emotional intelligence and selfless leadership. Here's how . . .

Emotional intelligence rests upon a foundation of empathy. Business leaders known for having high "EQs"—emotional quotients—do more than listen; they care. They walk in others' shoes readily, thereby making more thoughtful and deliberate decisions. They're known as excellent communicators, leaders who overcome challenges and defuse conflict. EQ leaders recognize that social skills are as, if not more, important than raw intelligence because effective leadership requires getting things done through others—not despite them.

Simply stated, emotional intelligence permits leaders to embrace nuances of human emotion in the workplace and can have pragmatic benefits, such as better collaboration among workers and a happier, lighter culture. EQ can be taught and improved, which is why emotional intelligence represents one of the hottest trends in leadership development today.

Leaders known for possessing high levels of EQ are self-aware and often have a reputation for creating friendly and inclusive work environments, recognizing and sharing their own shortcomings and limitations, making themselves vulnerable (in a healthy sense) to those whom they trust, letting go of mistakes and forgiving easily, neutralizing toxic people, and being good judges of character.

What might this look like in practical terms? EQ leaders pride themselves on being coaches and mentors to their team members, they believe in establishing goals and celebrating successes, and they constantly look for new ways to reinvent themselves in light of their organization's changing needs. They recognize that motivation is internal, and while they can't motivate others directly, they can create a work environment in which others can motivate themselves. In short, they come from gratitude and selflessness and embrace and inspire others by paying it forward.

Selfless leadership, also known as servant leadership, is a concept that goes back thousands of years but that was reinvigorated in 1970 in a book by Robert Greenleaf titled *The Servant as Leader*. Greenleaf's book stated, among other things, that the servant-leader is servant first. "It begins with the natural feeling that one wants to serve, to serve first. Then conscious choice brings one to aspire to lead." He then distinguishes between the leader-first and servant-first paradigms: "The difference manifests itself in the care taken by the servant-first to make sure that other people's highest priority needs are being served. The best test … is: Do those served grow as persons? Do they, while being served, become healthier, wiser, freer, more autonomous, more likely themselves to become servants? And what is the effect on the least privileged in society? Will they benefit or at least not be further deprived?"

Put another way, "If your actions inspire people to dream more, learn more, do more, and become more, than you are a leader." Commit to growing people and developing their talents. Enforce a performance management system that provides realistic developmental feedback to help others increase their self-awareness and prepare for their next move in career progression—whether at your firm or elsewhere. Help others codify their achievements and identify meaningful opportunities for growth. Hold others accountable to the highest standards of performance and conduct—not just for the sake of the organization but for their own professional development. You be the first domino. You demonstrate role model leadership so that others can emulate your example and respond in kind.

The business world doesn't need to be a shark tank. Create your own reality as you wish to live your life and experience your career. Authenticity, respect, and inclusion are your goals, tools, and opportunities. Use them to enrich people's lives and build stronger, better organizations. You'll likely find that others will gladly follow your lead and look to you for inspirational leadership.

INSPIRATIONAL LEADERSHIP

SOME FINAL THOUGHTS

Inspirational leadership is within your reach. It's not a far-off, idealistic fantasy. It's not about being a master communicator like Presidents Ronald Reagan or Bill Clinton. And it doesn't require extreme circumstances to reveal itself, like General George Patton in World War II. Instead, inspirational leadership reveals itself in many quiet ways, not only by what you do but, more importantly, by who you are.

We've discussed the concept that *beingness trumps doingness,* meaning that people respect you and are motivated and inspired by you primarily because of who you are as a leader, as a listener, and as a caring human being, not because of what you're doing at any given time. There's no need to try to figure out what to do, when in reality the simplest things, done in kindness and selflessness, help us stand out among our peers. Books on management offer hundreds or thousands of ways of motivating employees, but the truth is that workers motivate themselves. Your job is simply to create a work environment where they can do so. Discussions about motivation are typically called for at times of crisis: sudden spikes in turnover or rumors regarding union organizing activities—"Quick, get that book on motivation!" But wouldn't it be easier to come from the wisdom that says that creating the right environment from the outset is all that's really needed?

"What you want for yourself, give to another" is an additional workplace wisdom I mentioned earlier in this book—one that is sorely missing in corporate America. Unfortunately, law firms, accounting firms, and physician rotation and training programs speak proudly of their working newcomers to the bone. TV shows document and dramatize the effects of those twenty-four-hour shifts on young physicians' work lives and personal lives, while scientific and medical journals reflect the dangers of expecting young doctors to make life-altering decisions when sleep-deprived. "Track" career programs like these leave those who completed the program inflicting the same pain on new hires as they themselves experienced. And neither this book nor any other will likely change that survival-of-the-fittest mindset.

It doesn't have to be that way in your company, in your office, or on your shop floor. No matter where you work or what you do, you can be the best boss that your staffers have ever had. You can be that person who influenced and supported them to become better people and stronger contributors. You can be that caring person who encourages, that experienced mentor who guides, and that engaged leader who motivates.

It's easy to simply write off the idea of successful leadership. You may have not had particularly good bosses yourself throughout your own career. You may reason that you work in a cutthroat industry where everyone's out for him- or herself. And to a certain degree, this may be true. But that doesn't mean it has to be your reality or experience.

Change your perspective and you'll change your perception. Look at the world through a different lens and, while the objective outcomes of the reality surrounding you may not change, your experience of them can change immensely. This doesn't mean sticking your head in the sand and refusing to recognize reality. It does mean, however, that despite the dog-eat-dog nature of your industry, the craziness of your own leaders throughout your career, or the constant pressure you face to produce greater volumes at faster speeds, you can shield your people from those complexities. You can reason that the buck stops with you. You're the line of demarcation between the drama above you and what your team members get to experience under your leadership.

It all stems from simply changing your sponsoring thought about who you are as a leader, a motivator, and talent developer. Make it your goal to bring out the best in each of your subordinates—not to fix all their shortcomings but to harvest the best of the strengths that they have to offer. You know intuitively that successful leadership focuses on building on strengths rather than shoring up weaknesses, so find new ways of bringing out those strengths and inspiring employee engagement. Have fun. Consider lightening up just a bit. Understand that life is a gift, and for a significant portion of your lifetime, working with others will motivate you, frustrate you, engage you, and fascinate you.

Work, like life itself, is meant to touch all those feelings and emotions through your various experiences. But know that, at the end of it all, nothing will stick with you more than the people you've helped, the careers you've developed and built, and the people along the way who thanked you for all you did to help them excel and become their best. That's why leadership is the greatest gift that the workplace offers—because of its innate ability to help you touch lives and make the work world a better place.

■　■　■

That's the secret to all of this. That's the secret sauce of great leaders and inspirational leadership. It's not the end state—it's your trip along the way. Make the most of your career and your work life *through* people, not despite them. Teach what you choose to learn. Encourage others to take healthy risks. Be there when they make mistakes and offer support when they feel vulnerable. Understand that no one does anything wrong given their model of the world, and when in doubt, err on the side of compassion. You are the kind of leader you choose to be—the kind that can change people's lives and careers along the way. So go ahead and reinvent yourself. The world is waiting to see—and receive—that gift of leadership, of personal and career inspiration, and of selflessness that you are about to display. I hope this book helps you along the way.

INDEX

accountability, for perception management, 41–43

achievement calendar, quarterly, 50–51

achievement meetings, quarterly, 97–98

ADA (Americans With Disabilities Act), limitations of, 128–29

alignment of team, 64–65, 118

allyship, for diversity, equity and inclusion efforts, 109

American dream, 101

Americans With Disabilities Act (ADA), limitations of, 128–29

Angelou, Maya, 4

anger, coming from, 38–41

annual performance review, importance of, 15–16, 87

attitude problems, addressing, 42, 66–67

baby boomers, 101–2

bad news, delivering to employees, 38–39

balanced feedback, 13

"battle-buddy" relationships, 5

behavior
    addressing employee, 66–69
    ethical leadership, 9
    expectations for employee, 63, 83–85
    modeling leadership, 5, 17
    "silent," 66

"beingness," 3–4, 135

belonging, sense of, 26

best practices, for leadership, 6

board of directors, female director representation on, 109–10

boss, becoming a favorite, 3–9

Buckingham, Marcus, 36

business success
    establishing key metrics for, 113–18

calendar, quarterly achievement, 50–51

Calif., 109

career coaching language, 67

career development, 86–89

career growth, emphasize employee's, 21

Clinton, Bill, 135

coaching
    appropriate questions for, 12–16
    career language of, 67
    as leadership, 8–11
    to unlock others' potential, 87–89

Coffman, Curt, 36

collaborative work assignments, 104

collaborative work environment, 106

commitment, gaining verbal, 67–69

committee work opportunities, 105

communication
    challenges of, 58–61
    confrontation in, 57–63
    for constructive intervention, 64–69
    in difficult times, 5
    for employee development, 13–14
    for encouraging resignation, 70–77
    engaged listening for, 31–34
    formalizing the lines of, 48
    guidelines for, 35–43
    information sharing for, 49–51
    for leadership, 12–16

communication (*cont'd*)
multigenerational, 6
between multigenerational employees, 106
open lines of, 44
with remote employees, 95–99
skip-level meetings for, 52–56
in staff meetings, 44–48
community
creating social atmosphere of, 105
engagement in local, 109
completion notes, tracking, 49–50
conduct, 81–85
conduct infractions, 69
conformity, generational views on, 101
confrontation, 57–63
avoidance of, 57–58, 64–65
constructive, 65
judgment in, 65
structure of confrontive, 61–63
consensus, in leadership, 9
constructive confrontation, 65
constructive criticism, 45–46
constructive discharge claim, 71
continual feedback, 14
corporate social responsibility, 86, 109
COVID-19 pandemic, 90, 104
crises, strategies for management, 4–5
critical listening, 32
critical success factors (CSFs), 14
criticism, constructive, 45–46
curiosity, fostering, 23–24
customer satisfaction survey results (C-SAT), 22

decision-making, individual, 9
DEI. *see* diversity, equity and inclusion
delegation, 90–93
determination of suitability for, 92
to help others gain opportunities, 90–91
as mentoring exercise, 92–93

for proactive management, 93
selfless, 91
DeNiro, Robert, 104
developments, tracking, 49–50
dialogue, healthy group, 44
disability, perception of, 128–29
discretionary effort, from selfless leadership, 9
dispassionate players, in negotiation, 73
diversity, equity and inclusion (DEI), 86
incorporation of ideas of, 108–9
increasing awareness of, 6
for teambuilding, 107–10
documenting progress, for employee recognition, 6
documents, sharing, 49–50

EAPs (employee assistance programs), 127–28
"easy out" exit strategy, 73–75
education, for first-time managers, x–xi
effective listening, 32
emotional intelligence, 133
emotional quotients (EQs), 133
empathy
for emotional intelligence, 133
listening with, 32–34
employee accountability, 63
employee assistance programs (EAPs), 127–28
employee opinion survey, 22
employee recognition
documenting progress for, 6
importance of, 20–21
providing opportunities for, 21
Employee Resource Groups, 109
employees
building strengths of, 137
contributions of, at staff meetings, 45–46
crises of, 124–31
development of, 13–14, 22–23

disenfranchised, 70
dissatisfaction of, 120
engagement of, for employee retention, 23
importance of knowing names of, 21
including isolated, 124–27
motivation for, 5–6
multigenerational, 100–106
reducing turnover of, 119–23
relationships of, with supervisor, 36
remote, *see* remote employees
retention of, 23
soliciting input from, 122–23
employment defense attorney, working with, 71
engaged listening, 34
enlightened leadership, 77
environment
creating a welcoming, 21
for employee motivation, 135–36
environmental considerations, 114
environmentalism, 86
EQs (emotional quotients), 133
expectations
direct communication of, 63
resetting, 48

feedback
continual, 14
real time, 48
specific, 13
feelings, removing from confrontation, 63
female representation, on board of directors, 109–10
financial crises, 90
financial statements, 22
First, Break All the Rules (Buckingham and Coffman), 36
flexible work schedules, 104
Fortune 500, 108

Gallup organization, 36

Generation X, 100, 102
Generation Y, 102–3, 107. *see also* Millennials
Generation Z, 86, 105, 107
goal-setting, 87
Goldsmith, Marshall, 132
Greenleaf, Robert, 134
guilt, speaking from, 40–41, 68

HarperCollins Leadership Essentials, 108
Hathaway, Anne, 104
higher education, access to, 101
HR, working with
for reducing employee turnover, 119–23
when encouraging employee resignation, 71
human capital, key determinant of, 115–16
humor, appropriate workplace, 25–26. *see also* laughter, benefits of

implicit bias. *see* unconscious bias
incentives, experimental, 21
individual development plans (IDPs), 6
built around key business metrics, 113
quarterly, 87
quarterly meetings for, 15–16
industry-specific factors, 114
influence, calming, 5
information, sharing of, 49–51
informational listening, 32
innovation, laughter for, 26
insight, self-critical, 45
inspirational leadership, 17–19, 135–38
intermediaries, third-party, 73–77
The Intern (film), 104
internal promotion, 109
interventions
communication for constructive, 64–69
management, for alignment of team, 64–65

isolated employees, including, 124–27

judgment, in confrontation, 65

key metrics, 113–18
    individual development plans built
        around, 113
    problem solving with, 115–18
key performance indicators (KPIs), 22,
    114
key projects, tracking, 49–50

laughter, benefits of, 6, 25–28
leader-as-coach model, 11
leadership
    beingness for, 3–4
    and benefits of laughter, 25–28
    coaching as, 8–11
    communication for, 12–16
    concept of, 3–4, 8–9
    employee strength-building of, 137
    enlightened, 77
    gift of, xi
    inspirational, 17–19, 135–38
    mastering, 3–7
    remote, 94–99
    role model, 134
    selfless, see selfless leadership
    strengthening trust with, 20–24
    training workshop on, 104–5
    transparency for, 131
leading, by example, 17, 35
levity, and stress in the workplace, 25
limitations, self-imposed, 132
LinkedIn, 9, 11
listening, 31–34
    critical, 32
    effective, 32
    with empathy, 32–34
    to employees' input, 122–23
    engaged, 34
    informational, 32

macro level, of organizational impact, 46
management
    concept of, 3–4
    of crises, 4–5
    open-book, 22
    perception, see perception management
    proactive, 93
    self-assessment for effective, 132–34
    team-focused, 84–85
    traditional role of, 8–9
management by walking around (MBWA),
    21
management interventions, 64–65
managers, first-time
    education for, x–xi
    experiences of, ix–xi
MBWA (management by walking around),
    21
McKinsey and Company, 108
meetings
    having regular, with employees, 10
    quarterly, for individual development
        plans, 15–16
    quarterly achievement, 97–98
    quarterly one-on-one, 98
    skip-level, see skip-level meetings
    staff, see staff meetings
    weekly one-on-one, 95–96
    weekly team, 86
mentoring
    cross-generational, 104
    for diversity, equity and inclusion (DEI)
        efforts, 109
mentoring exercise
    delegation as, 92–93
metrics
    for employee motivation, 22
    key, 113–18
micro view, of work assignments, 46
Millennials, 86, 100, 105, 107
modeling, of behaviors, 4, 21
multigenerational communication, 6

multigenerational workforce, 100–106

negotiation, dispassionate players in, 73

objective observation, 65
one-on-one meetings
    quarterly, 98
    weekly, 95–96
open-book management (OBM), 22
open door policy, 19, 21
organizational factors, 114
organizational resources, 5
organizational strategy, staff recognition
    in, 20–21
"overmonitoring" employees, 120

parenting, 58–61
Patton, George, 135
perception management
    holding employees accountable for,
        41–43, 127
    of leadership, 66
performance
    and conduct, 81–85
    laughter for enhanced, 26
    managing, 64
    recognition of, 6
performance reviews, 87
    annual, 15–16
    increase number of, 12
personal relationships, building with
    employees, 36–38
perspective, changing, 5, 136–37
Pew Research Center, 100
phrasing, careful, 65–66
"please," importance of saying, 35
proactive management, 93
professional development, 86
    for employees, 17–18
    for teambuilding, 86–89
promotion, internal, 109
"psychic" income, of work, 92

quarterly achievement calendar, 50–51
quarterly achievement meetings, 97–98
quarterly meetings, for individual
    development plans, 15–16
quarterly one-on-one meetings, 98
questioning style, amending, 9–10
questions, importance of asking specific,
    19

Reagan, Ronald, 135
"rebel sales syndrome," 84–85
relationships, assessing, 17–18
remote employees
    feelings of being overlooked, 94
    performance level of, 94
    quarterly achievement meetings with,
        97–98
    quarterly one-on-one meetings with, 98
    supervising, 98
    weekly one-on-one meetings with,
        95–96
    weekly team meetings with, 86
remote leadership, 94–99
remote teams, workplace culture for, 28
resignation, encouraging, 70–77
resources, organizational, 5
respect
    importance of treating employees with,
        76
    work environment of, 22
retention efforts, 109
retirement, for baby boomers, 101–2
return to work, fitness-for-duty release
    for, 128
role model leadership, 134

safety, fostering feeling of, 127
schedules, flexible, 104
scorecards, 22
self-assessment, for effective management,
    132–34
self-critical insight, in staff meeting, 45

self-deprecating humor, 26
self-evaluations, annual, 87
self-imposed limitations, 132
selfless leadership, 4, 8–9, 18, 133–34
serious, corporate America as overly,
    26–27
The Servant as Leader (Greenleaf), 134
servant leadership. *see* selfless leadership
shared documents, 49–50
sincerity, for leadership, 8–9
skip-level meetings
    for communication, 52–56
    defined, 52
    expectations for, 53
    preparation for, 53–55
social community, creating, 105
social-networking tools, 106
Society for Human Resource Management,
    108
soft skills, importance of, 5
specific feedback, 13
staff meetings
    benefits of weekly, 46
    communication in, 44–48
    invitation for employees to contribute
        at, 45–46
staff recognition, 20–21, 44, 119, 125
staff updates, on current projects, 44–45
"stay interviews," 17–18
strategic considerations, in critical success
    factors, 114
strategies, for crises, 4–5
strength building, of employees, 137
stress in the workplace, levity for, 25
succession planning, 102, 105–6, 109
supervisor relationships, 36
support, proactively enlisting, 55–56
survival-of-the-fittest mindset, 136

teambuilding
    career and professional development
        for, 86–89

delegating for, 90–93
diversity, equity and inclusion for,
    107–10
for multigenerational employees,
    100–106
performance and conduct for, 81–85
for positive work environment, 104
remote leadership and, 94–99
team-focused management, 84–85
team meetings, weekly, 86
team players, characteristics of, 81–82
team turnarounds, 85
technologies, latest, 104
Tell the Truth (game), 27, 28
"thank you," importance of saying, 35
third-party intermediaries, 73–77
timely feedback, 13–14
touch-base meetings. *see* individual
    development plans
transparency, of leadership, 131
transparent communication
    for remote employees, 98
    with shared document, 50
trust, strengthening, 20–24

unconscious bias training, 109
upcoming events, tracking, 49–50
US Census Bureau, 100

verbal commitment, gaining, 67–69
veteran generation, 101
violence, threats of, 129–31
virtual employees. *see* remote employees

Walsch, Neale Donald, 4
weekly one-on-one meetings, 95–96
weekly team meetings, 86
What Got You Here Won't Get You There
    (Goldsmith), 132
work environment, positive, 104–5
workers, disenfranchised, 70
working conditions, 19–20

working relationships, 72
work-life balance, 86, 88, 94
workplace culture
  ideas for fun, 27–28
  for remote teams, 28
workplace violence, preventing, 124–31
work schedules, flexible, 104
wrongful termination and retaliation
  lawsuit, 76

"Yes . . . and" statements, 39
"Yes . . . but" statements, 39

Zoomers. *see* Generation Z

ABOUT THE AUTHOR

Paul Falcone (www.PaulFalconeHR.com) is the chief human resources officer (CHRO) of the Motion Picture and Television Fund in Woodland Hills, California, where he's responsible for all aspects of HR leadership and strategy. He's the former CHRO of the Nickelodeon Animation Studios and head of international human resources for Paramount Pictures in Hollywood. Paul served as head of HR for the TV production unit of NBCUniversal, where he oversaw HR operations for NBC's late night and primetime programming lineup, including *The Tonight Show*, *Saturday Night Live*, and *The Office*. Paul is a renowned expert on effective interviewing and hiring, performance management, and leadership development, especially in terms of helping companies build higher-performing leadership teams. He also has extensive experience in healthcare/biotech and financial services across international, nonprofit, and union environments.

Paul is the author of a number of HarperCollins Leadership, AMACOM, and SHRM books, many of which have been ranked on Amazon as #1 bestsellers in the areas of human resources management, labor and employment law, business mentoring and coaching, communication in management, and business decision-making and problem-solving. Bestselling books like *101 Tough Conversations to Have with Employees*, *101 Sample Write-Ups for Documenting Employee Performance Problems*, and *96 Great Interview Questions to*

Ask Before You Hire have been translated into Chinese, Vietnamese, Korean, Indonesian, and Turkish.

Paul is a certified executive coach through the Marshall Goldsmith Stakeholder Centered Coaching program, a long-term contributor to SHRM.org and *HR Magazine*, and an adjunct faculty member in UCLA Extension's School of Business and Management, where he's taught courses on workplace ethics, recruitment and selection, legal aspects of human resources management, and international human resources. He is an accomplished keynote presenter, inhouse trainer, and webinar facilitator in the areas of talent management and effective leadership communication.